Towards Wisdom

Sheila Ward

Towards Wisdom

*Elders Exploring Life Experience
to Create a Future of Hope*

Sheila Ward

First published 2007
This edition 2011

© Sheila Ward 2007, 2011

www.sophiatree.co.uk

Sheila Ward has asserted her right
under the Copyright, Design and Patents Act, 1988,
to be identified as Author of this work.

Without limiting the rights under copyright
reserved above, the author is happy
for her work to be used freely as appropriate.

The Author has made every attempt to contact copyright
holders but if any have been inadvertently overlooked she will
be pleased to make the necessary arrangements.

ISBN 978-1-907110-28-3

Produced by The Medlar Press Limited, Shropshire.

DEDICATION

*I dedicate this book to Alec, my generous,
honest and loving husband for more than
half a life-time, with my deepest
love and gratitude.*

*Also to our friends and family with whom
we have shared so much of our lives.*

*To my parents and grandparents who, by their love,
enabled my own explorations.*

*To Rosemary Ward, (my friend and colleague in
Women Exploring the Second Half of Life)
and to the many women who have
shared their life experience.*

My love and gratitude.

*It is dedicated, too, in hope and blessing,
to all the children of the world.*

Acknowledgements

My thanks to those who have read the first draft of this book and have given a helpful response without necessarily agreeing with what I have written. This enabled me to rewrite it in a more mature way: Ursula Dickenson, Moyna Lynch, Judith Hanmer, Susan Hannis, Beth Harris, Margaret Howlem, Sue Howse, Marie Miller, Jane Ozanne, Liz Perkins, John Pierson, Kate Porteus, Judith Smith, Elizabeth Staveley Gray, Angela Stewart, Rosemary Ward, Mike Ward, Anthony Ward, Jenny Dewar, Rosie Ward-Allen.

My thanks also to Ursula Dickenson and Kate Money who first initiated me into the ritual and sacredness of the 'circle'.

To Ursula King for her inspiring foreword to this second edition.

To Donald Reeves who by his courage and vision while Rector of St James Piccadilly enabled many new shoots of truth and love to emerge of which our women's circles was one.

To my many yoga teachers and especially to Lily de Speville (my first teacher), to Ruth White and to Danielle Arin (Lessware), who has generously allowed me to include (as an appendix) her contribution to our session at St James'.

To June Watts who introduced me to circle dance and for many years opened our year at the Grange with an inspiring weekend.

To Meg Wilkes who has provided counselling at our exploration weekends and to Ali McInroy who has provided a variety of therapies.

To Margaret Bailey who was a psychiatric social work tutor - a long-standing family friend and godmother to our youngest (but in practice to all our children). I would arrive, at her door energised, enthusiastic and hungry (especially after our sessions at St James' and a two hour yoga lesson) and she would provide me with an excellent meal and then lend an appraising ear to what I had been doing. Nourishing and grounding!

To Rosie and Jon Ward-Allen for their help in publishing this book and for enabling the continuation of the Exploring weekends at the Grange.

And to many other friends, too numerous to mention, who have helped in so many different ways.

The Author would like to thank the following for use of copyright material: Stephanie Sorrell, Betty James, Danielle Arin (Lessware), Frederica Chapman, Marianne Williamson (for extracts from her book A Return to Love*), Faber and Faber (for extracts from T. S. Eliot's 'Little Gidding'), Adrian Smith, Andrea Freeman, Jenny Joseph for 'When I am an Old Woman'.*

CONTENTS

I welcome the opportunity to write a foreword for this inspiring book. Here is a rich narrative of life's experiences gathered in through reflective meditation and dialogue with others. So much of the depth and beauty, but also the questions and struggles of the human search for meaning and harmonious relationships can be found in these pages that offer a wealth of challenging ideas to their readers.

Following the thread of her own life and gathering in some of its most significant moments, Sheila Ward takes us on an inner and outer exploration that opens up some amazing, new perspectives. The inspiring powers of wisdom and love at the centre of her story engage our body, mind and heart. Love and wisdom have been known to humans since ancient times; myriad religious and secular books sing their praise. But today, when humanity is at an important evolutionary juncture, we need to discover new ways that can help us in shaping our future development. This means to be open to forward thinking and courageous adventure, and to be committed to responsible action.

Among the many beautiful ideas in this book three appeal to me above all. The first is the wealth of wisdom hidden away untapped in people now in their second half of life, or what is sometimes even called its third or fourth stage. With the amazing growth in the number of people belonging to this group, we now possess for the first time an unprecedented, very large reservoir of human beings that, collectively, can mine a wealth of wisdom from the insights and experiences of their own lives. Sheila Ward argues, rightly in my view, that if we drew more creatively and imaginatively on these resources, we could access levels of insight and wisdom that greatly nurture and strengthen our life's possibilities and our relationships with other human beings. She has explored this experimentally through forming 'Wisdom Circles' and running a retreat centre for more than twenty years. These ventures bring together many people, especially women, in their second half of life who discover wisdom through accessing and sharing their own life stories while exploring their spirituality and creativity. These Wisdom Circles are linked to Sophia, the great female wisdom figure of ancient times that appeals to so many. Often seen as divine, she attracts many women and men, but especially feminist thinkers in different religions and cultures today.

The second idea that engages me greatly is not only Sheila Ward's emphasis on lived wisdom, but especially on the wisdom of women. She writes that 'Never before have there been so many old people in the world and never before has the world been in such need of their wisdom - a wisdom born of fifty, sixty, seventy or more years of life experience', and also that 'Women, particularly have a new and urgent role to play'. There is a Jungian emphasis on the feminine here, and an acute awareness of the spiritual and emotional creativity that can emerge in the second half of life. Many other women writers - novelists, psychotherapists, feminist philosophers and theologians among others, as well as women artists - have explored the decisive contribution that women, and especially older women, can and must make if people and planet are to have a worthwhile future that can ensure human happiness, dignity and cooperation.

This book is particularly written for women who 'have at least fifty years of life experience under their belt', but its message is not exclusively for them, since men and the young are equally in need of finding their way to wisdom at a time when great changes are happening in the world. Yet even more radical changes are urgently required if this world is to become a better place for all, and not just for the few.

Reflecting on women's wisdom makes me think of the eminent ecological thinker, Thomas Berry, who speaks about 'the great work' we have to do to bring about so many urgently needed changes in the pattern of our lives and in the structure of our institutions. He also says that we cannot accomplish such an enormous task without drawing on all the available sources of wisdom to guide us into the future. Among the four-fold sources of wisdom he mentions, the wisdom of women is one. The other three are the wisdom of indigenous people, the wisdom of the classical religious and philosophical traditions, and the newly discovered wisdom of science. Most of these have been neglected so far; the wisdom of women has certainly long been ignored or suppressed. This book provides a welcome antidote to such neglect, for it stresses the urgent and essential contribution that women and their newly articulated wisdom will make to our evolutionary leap forward into the future.

The third idea of great appeal is the discovery of how the path towards wisdom leads to and discloses an immense potential for a greater, deeper, more universal and all-inclusive love that can transform the world and energise us into new being and action. Sheila Ward calls this 'inspirational love' that brings head and heart together and goes far beyond the attraction of individual personal love, and also beyond the traditional bonds of friendship and community.

She is inspired by the powerful, transformative fire of this love. Initially rooted in personal experience, her reflections on love were further ignited and greatly inspired by the famous saying of the French priest and scientist, Pierre Teilhard de Chardin, who wrote in 1934: 'Some day, after mastering the winds, the waves, the tides, and gravity, we shall harness for God the energies of love, and then, for a second time in the history of the world, humanity will have discovered fire.'

This is a powerful invitation to a new awakening. Others have felt this too, and have been similarly moved to explore how we can harness the energies of love in a more effective and practical way for the common good of ourselves and our communities. How to nurture, develop and practise a stronger, richer, more holistic love? A love that is linking and bonding, healing and strengthening, but also a love that can be strong and tough at times. A love that is not primarily an emotion, but a tremendous power, a fiery energy that leads us into befriending ourselves, each other, and the Earth. It has been said that 'those who live the mystery of love are lights, carriers of fire and conduits of power' (Anne Hillman).

Sheila Ward has captured so much of this fire that she realises that much traditional talk on love seems to be more 'like the waters of life iced over'. Awakening the energies of love means living in relationship, and focussing on the energies that operate between us in different kinds of relationships. Extending our relationships into ever wider circles we come to realise how we are connected to the greater community of life. We therefore need a much larger vocabulary to talk about love, and have to learn to increase our capacity to love. This means also re-examining the assumptions embedded in our forebears' thinking about love.

These great themes offer a rich tapestry of a life-enhancing spirituality whose threads run through the entire book, complemented by a whole chapter devoted to this central, urgent concern. Spirituality relates to all human life, to embodiment, to health and education, to our experience of birth, life and death, but also to our global world with its great diversity of peoples and beliefs. Other aspects of spirituality connect with gender, world faiths, a new ecological consciousness, an emerging global ethic, and the power of meditation and prayer. These and many others themes are touched upon in this book.

Spirituality is not just about personal inner development, but it must encompass the flourishing of all people and the planet in a new way, and embrace the whole of life. This requires the bringing together of the best of the past with the urgent needs of the present and future. Sheila Ward's book helps us to seek life in abundance for a new season of the world. She asks 'What makes your heart sing?' and 'What makes you fully alive?', for what the world needs most are people who are truly alive.

At the heart of this is the energy of love that sustains all life. The encouraging thoughts of this book do much to help us gain access to these life-sustaining and life-transforming sources of energy. I sincerely hope that many people will benefit from its wisdom and be empowered to work for the personal and social transformation so urgently needed in our world today.

Ursula King
Author of *The Search for Spirituality.*
Our Global Quest for Meaning
and Fulfilment (2009)

The concept of evolution has changed our perspective on life - yet the main interest still lies in how humanity has developed up to now. But what next? Evolution is not going to stop. Where do we go from here? Over thousands of years man has developed many faculties. Who can tell at present what unknown potential may lie within us and which we may be able to develop?

Darwin's first criteria for evolutionary development was 'survival of the fittest' but today humanity makes a conscious choice to look after its least fit. Our self-awareness has reached a point where we can all, not just the scientists, look for growth points in the human personality that can lead to a transformation of life and society.

Nearly a hundred years ago Teilhard de Chardin, a priest and palaeontologist foretold an evolutionary leap. At that time his ideas were rejected but now there are many small groups exploring what such ideas could mean. It is difficult to imagine how humanity could further evolve and essentially we are moving into an unknown future. (He also foretold a 'linking of minds' and so may have been one of the few people who foresaw the internet which in itself could be part of an evolutionary leap.) He associated such a leap especially with women and this could be because, for thousands of years women's life experience and spirituality have been suppressed under a mostly patriarchal society.

It seemed that this might in part explain why, although there has been enormous material progress over the last several thousand years, we humans are still emotionally much as we ever were and it is assumed to be a fundamental truth that 'You can't change human nature'. Perhaps it could change if women's wisdom was taken into account?

Over the last fifty years or so women's wisdom circles have been proliferating across the world as women told their stories and women novelists wrote about life from a woman's point of view.

I felt sure that there was a huge spiritual potential among older women which as yet was largely untapped. So for the last twenty years I have been exploring this with women who have had at least fifty years of life experience, ie, women in the second half of life. All women are different but over these years it has become apparent that most women are much more comfortable than men in exploring emotional matters such as love; they cooperate rather than compete and they have a different attitude to sexuality.

I wrote the first edition of this book on the basis of those explorations. But now we need men's wisdom too.

Some of those who have been exploring the possibility of an evolutionary leap now suggest that it may be at a stage of development in which the 'me, me, me' of our present culture is superseded by an awareness of community needs and the needs of the world. We no longer seek for 'my happiness', 'my well being' - not because of any denial of self , but rather by expanding our love and awareness so that we seek the happiness and well-being of our community, the whole world and future generations. Some call this a 'shift of consciousness' which is already happening. Numerous small enterprises are changing the world. A need is identified and new initiatives taken together to bring about a more creative and joyful world for future generations. This is a movement with no leaders. and no ideology. It ties in with the search for a global spirituality - the realisation that we are all interdependent - that we are all one. However, this involves a new emotional maturity so we need to understand much more about love.

One of the experiences which is helping to bring this about is the phenomenon of what is variously known as 'Realisation', a 'mystical',' transpersonal' or a 'peak' experience. This is being experienced by an increasing number of people. It may happen fleetingly for only a few moments or it may be much longer, in which case it changes lives. It is an ecstatic sense of being part of a much bigger whole. There is a complete loss of ego but a huge energy and vastly increased capacity to love. Not everyone will know what I am talking about. It does not seem to fit the pattern of our everyday life which is perhaps why those who have had such an experience do not talk about it. Another reason is that it is so special that it almost seems sacrilegious to mention it to anyone who would not understand. Yet such experiences are becoming more frequent and by their very nature seem part of a world which is bigger than the present one.

A second such experience is the phenomenon of 'falling in love'. We use this word for a number of different experiences some of which may simply be a fleeting physical attraction. But we also use this same phrase 'falling in love' for what may be the basis of a lifelong partnership - or the devotion of a poet to his muse (in which there may be no physical relationship). However it happens, this state of 'being in love' is imbued with an ecstasy which is beyond our normal everyday experience. What does this mean?

Love is not something which can be learnt from books. However, it may be learnt from example and from wisdom based on more than half a lifetime's experience. Older people need to explore their experience of love - or lack of it - so that we may then share our experience with the next generation, many of whom have never been loved.

If this is to happen, the best tool we have at present is the enormous number of reading circles which already explore experiences of love vicariously and may include both men and women.

Although this second edition is intended for both men and women readers, I have retained most of the material from our original explorations.

I think that women's wisdom circles will continue to proliferate, so I am leaving the chapter which describes how such a circle may be set up. (Indeed there are some aspects of this which may also be relevant for reading groups.) The exploration of Authenticity may perhaps spark off thoughts about male authenticity. I hope our exploration of spirituality may be of interest to both men and women. The account of ways for marking a woman's life cycle might perhaps find reciprocal ideas for men, especially the urgent need to discover ways for bringing our young into the responsibility of adult life.

We can only build up wisdom from our own life experience and each of us is different so my own life story is only relevant as being the starting point for this book.

I hope that the final two chapters on 'Love' and 'Hope for the Future' will provide material for an exploration which will carry us forward.

Whether they like it or not future generations can only start from the base of their ancestors. We may be trying to save the planet but concern for future generations requires much more than ecological solutions. Maybe the young have overtaken us by their knowledge of new technology. But this could be part of the problem. The head has outrun the heart, and life experience is too easily discounted. Truth has many facets and everyone can contribute their experience and interpretation. Such contributions may vary radically but by sharing and honouring such experience and insights with each other our awareness may increase and our understanding deepen

I hope this book may be used as a tool by older men and women speaking from the heart from their own experience and that it may lead to the germination of seeds which at present are mostly below the surface. We need to let go of certainties and find new perspectives and horizons. There are experiences in life which we do not understand and so mostly do not talk about, but which could be very important for future development and could lead to greater understanding, a new emotional maturity and ultimately a whole new way of being.

Sheila Ward
June 2011

1

INTRODUCTION:
FINDING OUR WAY TOWARDS WISDOM

The wise stand out,
Because they see themselves as part of the Whole.
They shine,
Because they don't look for recognition.
Their wisdom is contained in what they are,
Not their opinions.

Lao Tzu's Tao Te Ching

The future of humanity lies in the hands of those who are
strong enough to provide coming generations with reasons
for living and hoping.

Adrian Smith

I am daughter, sister, mother in thousands of generations of
women, women whose skills created peaceful and beautiful
civilisations, women who preserved remnants of our knowledge
when the civilisations passed. I am a woman. In me lives the
knowledge and experience of all beings. I can use that knowledge
and experience to create a loving, spontaneous world.

Ann Valliant

We live in a time of great change - a time of rapid scientific and technological advancement: we travel in space, we trade across the world, we have the power to create life and the power to destroy it - in vast numbers. There is a great respect for the technicians, the scientists, the businessmen who have the energy and imagination to venture ever further along this seemingly one-way track. There is also adulation of sportsmen and 'celebrities' which combines with a cult of youth to provide young people with more money and power than ever before. But there is something else new about our society today, an asset that has not been recognised and which, perhaps more than anything else, holds the key to our future life on Earth, and that is the asset of an aged population. Never before have there been so many old people in the world and never before has the world been in such need of their wisdom - a wisdom born of fifty, sixty, seventy and more years of life experience.

Women, particularly, have a new and urgent role to play. Jung pointed out that woman is the only female on the planet whose active life continues beyond the time of her potential for giving birth. He thought this had some evolutionary significance. Now, as never before, we are living for a long time beyond the menopause with good health, wide experience and the opportunity for further training and education. For the first time in our history we have the opportunity, as older women, to follow a dream, share a vision and co-create a world for future generations. What if the potential for physical creativity flips over at the menopause into the potential for spiritual and emotional creativity? And what if we can harness that potential? Could we, indeed, change the world we live in and become an evolutionary force in our society? I think so, and I hope to be able to persuade you to think so too. But is anything happening already, you may ask? And what do we mean by wisdom?

This book is written for women with at least fifty years' life experience under their belt. It is only our life experience which can give us the basis for wisdom. I can affirm and begin to understand this by listening to the experience of others. There are many situations of confidentiality where this can happen. Recently it has been possible for many of us to find such a tool for listening in 'Wisdom Circles'.

My own background is Christian, although it is simply Christ's words 'Love one another as I have loved you' and 'I came that ye might have life and have it more abundantly' which I find relevant to my life today. I have learnt much from other religions and hope I still continue to learn.

I have always been interested in the truth about 'love' - that umbrella word which has so many different meanings. This led me to question the nature of life itself and to wonder whether other women had had any similar experiences to mine and felt the same way as I did. Later on I began exploring this, with women who had at least half a life-time's experience behind them, and to look for somewhere where such groups could meet in peaceful surroundings to share their stories and their feelings about life. In 1987 we found a place. This was a country house in Shropshire called 'The Grange', and it is mainly there that these groups have met.

I have written this book primarily for such women, but I hope that it may also be of interest to both men and women who are exploring our way forward into the future.

When our explorations began I was not sure what would emerge. However after twenty years I think it is becoming clearer and I would like to encourage other women to share their life experience. So when I speak of 'our experience' or tell you that 'we' found it helpful, I am referring to the groups which have been ongoing over the last twenty years. Not every-one will agree with our findings, nor were they necessarily unanimous, but this is all part of the exploration. I suspect that it is the process rather than any 'results' which matter.

This is a book about 'circles' of women exploring to find wisdom. So let us look and see what it could mean. What is wisdom? Why women? And what are 'circles'?

What is Wisdom?

'I'll give you a nugget of wisdom,' we say, going on to produce some platitudinous adage which may have been passed on to us as a child. Because of our deference to our elders, especially in the past, we tended to look back for a wisdom which may have been culled and passed on through the centuries by our ancestors. But while much of what passes for wisdom may have been brilliant advice at the time, it is often not relevant to our world today. There may seem to be 'ancient precepts' that one might think could have eternal value, such as 'Speak the truth' and 'Love one another' but even here we have to ask what we actually mean by 'truth' and even more what we mean by 'love'.

Perhaps the main thing I have learnt during my own explorations is that wisdom does not lie in structures of belief but in the way that we live our lives.Our way of life may, it's true, be influenced to some extent by our belief system. For example, if I believe that the most significant part of my life exists after my death then I may be motivated to 'do good' but may be less interested in preserving life on this planet. On the other hand, if I care passionately about my children and future generations and believe that the human race is capable of evolutionary transformation then I shall be concerned to keep an open mind and learn how to love more fully in relationship with my fellow human beings. Perhaps we should think of wisdom as not so much to do with discovering a higher, wider knowledge, but as something we gain by making us more mature.

There is a story of a man who was given the task of making a whole garden silver. He bought some pots of silver paint and slaved away for weeks. Finally he gave up. Then that night the temperature dropped and the garden was instantly transformed into a silver wonderland; a change in the climate had brought about what years of slow toiling could never effectively achieve. It is something akin to this which needs to happen to our world today - a change of emotional and spiritual climate.

The thinking which now shapes our Western civilisation is centred on the self. Modern psychology focuses on self-sufficiency, the pursuit of happiness and more recently on personal growth (although we know that this cannot happen in isolation). In Christianity, although Christ's main teaching was that we should love one another, the focus too often shifts on to personal salvation and our life in the hereafter. Our psychology and religion are focussed on the individual human being, too often in isolation, and however positive and life enhancing this may have become in recent years, the urgent need now seems to be to re-focus on the energies and magnetism operating *between* us. We need to focus on love and on a vision of how the future could be for all humanity.

For a long time in our history, women, as children and growing adults, absorbed without question not only factual knowledge but theories and ideas about the meaning of life. But during the last century women have at last learnt how to think for themselves and to explore a new understanding of life. Even so, some of the beliefs in which we were brought up are so deeply embedded that we may not even be aware that they are there. As Jung said, 'It is hard to look at the lion that has swallowed you'. Our lives are filled with innumerable basic assumptions which we need to identify and then question.

There is so much unknown and so much to which we are oblivious. We may not be able to hear the squeaking of a bat or the whistle which brings a dog to heel because such sounds are beyond the scope of our hearing - but, thanks to modern science, we know they are there. Likewise, the uninitiated are unaware of radio-waves, hydrogen or the potential of energy in oil. And there must be so much more that we have not yet discovered. The more we understand, the larger is our circumference of the unknown.

On the other hand there is much that we do not see but which we *could* see if it was pointed out to us. My uncle was a medical researcher and spent most of his life trying to identify and isolate the cause of a tropical disease. Finally it was discovered by someone else. He looked back through his slides and immediately saw that the solution had been there time and again, but until he had the eyes of knowledge he had not been able to see it. In biology classes a dye is often injected into the slide so that vital tissue can be identified which would otherwise have passed unnoticed. When a previously unnoticed element in our surroundings is pointed out, it can change our whole perception of the world.

Why Women?

This book deals a lot with exploring and articulating emotional issues and this is something which, on the whole, women seem to be much more comfortable with than men, at least men of my generation.

This is probably a cultural matter of upbringing, but may also be partly due to the fact that women are biologically tied into the very fabric of the universe - our bodies responding to the moon and the tides as well as experiencing the very physical event of childbirth. Women also usually take the major share of bringing up small children as well as caring for the sick and the dying. Increasingly men are beginning to share in such experiences but as a woman of my generation I am writing this book for those who are among the elders now (although I hope it may be of interest to all who are interested in the future of the world).

For thousands of years our theories about the meaning of life have been dominated by male thinking, and it is only recently that 'women's values' have come to the fore and have enabled a new perception. Although the world will surely need the talents and understanding of both men and women if we are to create a place where children can grow in love, freedom and hope, we need to appreciate that there *is* a difference between the male and the female way of thinking and operating. On the whole, men seem to feel more comfortable with ideas which involve analytical and left-brain thinking, and with a hierarchical pattern of action.

Women are perhaps more naturally curious than men. We ask questions and even more think questions which we do not always voice. 'Why is the sky so blue?' 'How do swallows find their way to Africa?' 'Why have I fallen in love with him? - or her?' Sometimes there may be a scientific answer and sometimes not. We need to explore much more on the heart level. And we may find that, as we explore, we see the whole world in a completely new way, and develop a new paradigm. We may find a meaning which we had not suspected.

Both men and women can feel a natural affinity with the mountains, the seas, the birds, animals and flowers. Wordsworth wrote:

> . . . *And I have felt*
> *A presence that disturbs me with the joy*
> *Of elevated thoughts; a sense sublime*
> *Of something far more deeply interfused,*
> *Whose dwelling is the light of setting suns,*
> *And the round ocean and the living air,*
> *And the blue sky, and in the mind of man;*
> *A motion and a spirit, that impels*
> *All thinking things, all objects of all thought,*
> *And rolls through all things.*

On a mountain, beside the sea, reading such poetry, we instinctively recognise a deep truth, yet we return to a world built up on alien patterns of thought and behaviour. Both men and women experience awe and ecstasy but I think there is a difference between the male and female experience. As a preliminary observation I would suggest that for men such experience seems to evoke the response of seeking for something higher than our present life, perhaps 'salvation'? 'enlightenment'? 'God'? For women (for myself at least) it evokes a feeling of oneness and a passion for ensuring that such a beautiful world can be a place where my children, grandchildren and children of future generations can live and love and grow. We need to discover the significance of these experiences.

We shall explore these ideas further in the chapter on 'Authenticity' where we shall examine concepts which were formed centuries ago and have continued unquestioned into our present time - concepts such as those which emerged during the overthrow of Sumer:

Sumer and its lasting effects[1]

History books tell us that our Western society has been continuously patriarchal, with men in charge of everything and women having an inferior status. However, comparatively recent excavation suggests that there was a society before recorded history which reached an outstanding degree of development, where men and women were genuinely equal.

Sumer, with its goddess Inanna, the radiant queen of Heaven and Earth, was a city state in Mesopotamia roughly in the area where Iraq lies today. Two major developments occurred here - developments which altered the course of human history: firstly, animals and plants began to be grown systematically for food about 7500 BC and secondly, the fundamental arts of civilisation - writing, maths, architecture, astronomy, government and temple worship - all came into being around 3500 BC. These people may have invented the wheel. The first known written language may also have developed here although there is no recorded evidence.

Reading between the archaeological lines, there was a creative partnership in Sumer between men and women. Sexuality was sacred. Men as well as women were loving and helped in the upbringing of children (as many men do today) but they acknowledged the difference between them and respected each other's special strengths and skills. Women participated fully in sacred activities, owned property and business and if they were unmarried could serve as priestess-physicians. They were also able to be scribes, thus recording the culture through their own experience. Men, it seems, found this liberating, finding greater fulfilment in love rather than in power.

The biological aspects of procreation were understood and it was known that children could not be conceived without the male and female. Reflecting this knowledge, their creation myths involved both sexes, with the female giving birth to the world. In Sumer the most sacred of all acts - the sexual union - was celebrated as the spring came. The union of male and female was enacted to encourage the birth and growth of all that sustained life. It was an act representing love, healing and birth - the trifold concern of Inanna. Ishtar was another compassionate healing goddess. Some sources refer to this people as having a 'religion of ecstasies'.

Then in about 2600 BC came the invasion of other tribes with a dominant male god. The land of Sumer became a battlefield and it was to Ishtar that supplications were made. She became the goddess of war and slowly, insidiously there crept in more praises for her sexuality and fewer for her healing nature.

In the 'Epic of Gilgamesh' written in about 2000 BC, King Gilgamesh calls Ishtar 'a predatory and promiscuous woman'. In retaliation Ishtar threatens to unleash the bull of Heaven. The goddess of all things light and dark became the wild goddess of the terrible.

The Istaritu were holy women of the temple who represented Ishtar in the act of consummating the sacred marriage. In early times they embodied the essence of the deity and showered blessing upon the men who sought their presence. As the perception of Ishtar became increasingly more sexual and more promiscuous, so the holy women were increasingly transformed into harlots associated with decadence and orgies, devoid of any holy significance. All of this accompanied the demise of the Sumerian civilisation which ended about 1000 BC in disorder, injustice and inequality. Women were excluded from education. By 700 BC they could no longer be scribes or doctors, and participation in the healing arts had been downgraded to one of service only. Although women were still acting as midwives, this profession had lost stature because procreation and birth were seen less as a miracle and more as a shameful, degrading activity. By 1000 BC the Mother goddess had been replaced in the records of the Near East by a male god, usually of wind, air or thunder. The goddesses became wives and daughters.

Until the last known burning of a witch at the end of the eighteenth century, women with the gift of healing were often perceived as witches, tortured and burned. Such delusions sprang from a distorted understanding of life, stemming from a mythology centred on an arrogant, judgemental and vindictive father god. The advent of Christ who treated men and women as equal and urged us to love one another might have ushered in a new way of living, but it was soon overtaken by the old beliefs. Too often Christ's promises of forgiveness, love and healing were translated by power-hungry men into guilt, suffering and sacrifice.

The creativity of men and women in the Sumerian civilisation seems to indicate that there was a time when men and women lived in tune with themselves and with each other but, as their civilisation disintegrated, both men and women developed false perceptions of each other and of themselves which still echo down the centuries.

All this goes back a long way and more recently women in some parts of the world have once more begun to live in equality with men but there is still much healing needed in the relationship between them and in our understanding of sexual union.

Of course, not all men and women through the ages shared this false perception. There have been *some*, away from the mainstream of events who have lived peaceful lives in love and partnership. Indeed, there were movements running counter to these old beliefs that emerged during the nineteenth and twentieth centuries: Quakers and Methodists in the field of Christian religion, suffragettes in the field of politics, and others in medicine, science and other areas of life - movements that are well known and have paved the way for a more comprehensive understanding of what it is to be a man - and a woman - and for considering the nature of love.

(There is also a need for more understanding of gay relationships, but my concern in this chapter and the next is simply to free women from the misperceptions of the past.)

The Two Trees in the Garden of Eden [2]

The three religions of our Western world, Christianity, Islam and Judaism, all with their male God all recount the creation story of the Garden of Eden. There were two trees growing in this garden: the Tree of Knowledge and the Tree of Life. Until recently the Tree of Life has been mostly forgotten, whereas the Tree of Knowledge has been a source of guilt, conflict, misery and death. The story of this tree must surely be an allegorical, intuitive account of humanity's emergence into consciousness and speech. As they slowly acquired knowledge, men developed different perceptions of the truth. There is a well known story of blind men trying to describe an elephant when one has hold of its trunk, another its leg, another its ear and another its tail, and they produce widely differing descriptions of 'the truth' of what an elephant is. In the same way, man's increasing knowledge, developing as it did from different starting points, led to conflict. Throughout history, people have been killed because someone else wanted to impose on them their concept of 'the truth' instead of recognising how much we do not know. Obviously it is not knowledge itself which has been the cause of death but rather the arrogance of thinking that partial knowledge was the whole and then trying to make everyone else think the same way.

The Tree of Knowledge grew and flourished. In addition the hierarchical way of operating required total obedience and for centuries female questioning was not tolerated.

Now we need to cultivate the Tree of Life[3] and in this women have a major role to play. That is not to say that women are lacking in knowledge - far from it. But maybe we are more prepared to sit with the unknown and with paradox and to explore our emotional life. The Tree of Life has been sadly neglected. Doesn't abundance of life depend on abundance of love? How much do we understand about our emotions? About the magnetism between us? About the dynamics of love?

Popular Psychology

It was only a little more than a hundred years ago that the emotional life began to be taken seriously, but it was only those with problems who went to the early psychologists (who were all male). These psychologists built up their theories on the basis of patient records, producing assumptions that everyone is, at one level or another, motivated by self interest. This is widely accepted by popular psychology today although in recent years many other more advanced but lesser known theories have been suggested.

Could such theories, originally designed to cure problems, have actually moulded behaviour? It seems likely, but the implicit assumptions about human nature are limited and do not allow for the growth of which humanity is capable. Those affected by these assumptions may, in fact, be stunting their emotional growth.

On the other hand, I suspect that there are many happy, healthy families who have never come within the purview of the academic psychologist. That is not to say that they have not had their fair share of troubles but because they have been spared the worst ravages of war, and have not been influenced by some of the current trends in thought and behaviour, they have a natural enthusiasm for life, are keen to learn, responsive to need and reaching out in love to their fellow human beings with a sense of community. This is their natural behaviour which may sometimes be disrupted but suggests to me that all human beings could naturally behave like this if they were given love, affirmation, health and security from birth onwards. Such an assumption also raises the controversial issue of whether human nature is naturally good or not. This is far too simplistic and a dualistic way of thinking. We are all different and it could be better instead to ask what motivates us - which again has various sources. We may be driven by love for another, by a thirst for knowledge, by a response to need, by devotion to a cause etc. Self interest is surely one of these drives but by no means always the dominant one. Often we hear that 'human nature is "flawed"'. Might it not be better to say 'immature'?

Sophia

Wisdom has often been referred to down the centuries as 'Sophia' and because this is a woman's name we tend to think of her as representing women's wisdom and that is what this book is about. The aim is not to tell you anything but rather to ask you questions. I may make suggestions, but it is your response that matters. And there may not always be answers. Sometimes we come across something in our own experience or another's which we do not understand. Let's not rush in too hastily with an explanation. We are moving into uncharted waters and we may not even have a vocabulary to encompass what is puzzling us. We need to keep an open mind and just be aware of resonance. If we use the analogy of the butterfly it is worth remembering that during the time in chrysalis the larval framework is broken down while the adult structures of the insect are formed. So we need to let go of certainties and assumptions as we open ourselves to creativity. What will emerge is beyond our present comprehension.

Wisdom Circles

Each of us has a life-time of experience which is equally valuable. However, there is great diversity. I cannot be sure that something is true simply on the basis of my own experience. It needs to be compared with the experience of others.

Meeting 'in circle' comes naturally to women - here they can take joint responsibility and can listen to and share their stories. Over the past twenty years such circles have experienced a revival. In 1993 the 'International Women's Dialogues' took place in Boston, USA; in 1994 there was a gathering in New Zealand; and in 1995 the Global Women's Initiative was held in the UK. On a much larger scale there was the Beijing Conference of Women in 1995 and 'Women of Spirit' in South Africa in 1996. All these events spawned smaller women's circles especially in the USA and South Africa.

In the first chapter of this book I talk about the formation and guidelines for a 'Wisdom (or Sophia) Circle' based on the experience of our 'Second Half of Life' explorations. Women with half a life-time's experience behind them have a basis from which to explore and can more easily get away from books and theories (although obviously these can be illuminating as long as we question them as we go along).

When I first began exploring with groups of older women at the Grange, I was not sure what the outcome would be. We have been exploring there now for over twenty years and a wealth of life experience has been poured out. Sometimes someone will speak of an experience which they have never told anyone about before. This would not be a guilty secret but simply something which did not fit into the present framework of expectation. We need to include such seeds in our search for wisdom.

If I look at a seed or an egg, I could have absolutely no conception of what the end product would be unless I had seen it with my own eyes. Frequently, new growth comes from intuitive beginnings and often from the transformation of mistakes or misfortunes. I see 'Wisdom Circles' as the cells of a new embryo within a chrysalis which will eventually bring forth a butterfly with a whole new way of being.

For 'Sophia' is slow growing. I always expect that when someone finds a new way of looking at things, it will change their life at once and everything will be immediately different, but it takes time and cannot be rushed. The native American Indians advised their people to consider what effect their actions would have on those who followed them up to seven generations in the future. I find it difficult enough to get my head round the thought of my granddaughters' grandchildren - and, to follow the American Indian advice, there would still be three more generations to go after that! We need to be aware not only of the eternal dimension in 'Now' but also of the immensity of chronological time.

It has taken me over twenty years to be able to articulate an aspect of love which I knew intuitively so long ago and which I consider in the later part of the book. It is important to allow time for growth. It takes time, too, to build up a circle of trust and love in which precious and intimate experience can be shared. Many experiences cannot be spoken of without this. It is in vulnerability that love and growth develop.

It is also important, in our search for deeper meaning, that we approach it as sacred. This does not preclude laughter (who laughs more than the Dalai Lama?) but it means that there is a deep underlying seriousness in what we are doing as we search for truth.

'Sophia' has an open mind, a searching spirit and a loving heart. This book is written on the basis of circles we have convened mostly at the Grange on our three-day weekends and my own life experience.

The Format of the Book

I begin by describing the formation of a Wisdom Circle for those who do not already know.

The next chapter is concerned with finding our own authenticity and contains questions and suggestions for further exploration. It is unhelpful to set out on our journey with a false map of unverified assumptions.

By this time there will be an ethos of love and trust within the group and we may tell our life stories. So I tell my own story, the first part being up to the age of fifty and the second part relating to the second half of my life up to now. I hope the reader may find resonance. My own life has been richly blessed for which I am extremely grateful. It has undeniably been 'privileged', although not in the sense of wealth or power or celebrity. However, I have been loved since birth, and have lived in a safe environment, free from the damage of war, with no shortages of food, shelter or clothing, and given a liberal education. This has at least given me the opportunity to explore widely. Other lives which have been more scarred and wounded may have a deeper vein of wisdom to contribute, but will be much more painful to relate. I recognise this in all humility. Those who have lived in other cultures from my own may not relate in the same way to the same issues, but there will surely be resonance and it is only from a wide diversity of life experience that we can begin to discover true wisdom. Let us not be afraid to sit with paradox and apparent contradiction.

After 'My Story' I look at what we mean by 'Spirituality'. Spirituality is very closely associated with wisdom and it was on my quest for the reality of spirituality in our life today that I discovered Wisdom Circles and the beginnings of wisdom.

My experience has led me to the conclusion that the truth of 'Sophia' (woman's wisdom) lies in love. So this, above all, is a subject I feel we need to explore in great depth. Since my early days I have been interested in the various meanings of love and how we can learn to love. Increasingly I began to focus on the ubiquitous but little studied phenomenon of 'falling in love' - such a powerful force in our lives but one which is usually laughingly dismissed. This is one of the aspects which I explore in the chapter on 'Love' - the most important and almost the final chapter in the book. Almost - because the last part suggests a vision of the world which I see emerging when our work is done.

We have a task ahead of us indeed. And it will take time. Time to grow the Tree of Life.

2

FORMING A WISDOM CIRCLE

Somewhere there are people
to whom we can speak with passion
without having the words catch in our throats.
Somewhere a circle of hands will open to receive us,
eyes will light up as we enter, voices will celebrate with us
whenever we come into our own power.
Community means strength that joins our strength
to do the work that needs to be done.
Arms to hold us when we falter.
A circle of healing. A circle of friends.
someplace where we can be free.

Starhawk 'Dreaming the dark'

Don't withdraw from me, step towards me.
Don't shun me, embrace me.
Don't sue me, mediate with me.
Don't assume - question.
Don't let our difference blind us to our commonality.
Who knows what risks we will take if we are asked?
If the task is explained clearly,
If our contribution is valued,
If we can count on each other.

Christina Baldwin

The circle is there to remind us of who we truly are.

Beverly Engel

Forming a circle need not be a difficult operation. From a small
acorn an oak tree can grow! If you are hoping to form a circle,
then begin by discussing it with a friend. Each of you can then

think of others whom you could invite. The main criteria for participants would be the ability to be open, to be prepared to learn and practise listening skills, to be confidential and to give commitment.

Sometimes circles meet every month but one of our 'Friends of Sophia Circles' at the moment is meeting quarterly, while another is meeting every two months. If it is not too often it makes it easier to give commitment; on the other hand, if too infrequent, it may lose connection. Both the circles I've mentioned meet in somebody's home and it is important that this is a quiet place free from interruption. One group meets in the afternoon and the hostess provides tea and biscuits. The other, whose members are more far-flung, bring a packed lunch and stay for the best part of the day. The number of people participating would ideally be between six and twelve but it is possible to start with three or four and perhaps if numbers become too great then the group could divide.

The minimum time to allot would be about two hours, with an extra half hour beforehand for tea, biscuits and exchanging news before the session starts. It is an essential preparation time so that people do not come rushing in from the road straight into circle.

I very much recommend Christina Baldwin's book *Calling the Circle* and Beverly Engel's *Women Circling the Earth*. Both writers have a far wider experience of circle than I have and both books are inspiringly written. As a preliminary, however, I will tell you what we do at the Grange. This is simply an outline so feel free to take what you wish from our experience and leave the rest. Each circle is different.

Limbering Up

On our weekends we make sure that body mind and spirit are fully alert by doing some simple exercises before we begin. Then with feet planted firmly on the floor and the spine lifting

we just stand relaxed for a few minutes. After this we sometimes do deep breathing, taking the arms up as we breathe in
and rising on our toes; then out as we come down. We often
combine this with visualisation so that when we breathe in
someone says a word such as 'love', 'joy', 'peace', 'fully alive',
and then on the outbreath we feel the meaning of this word
flooding through us. Sometimes we do Tai Chi or yoga. Five
minutes will be enough and those who have problems with
movement can join in as much as possible and visualise.

After this we bring the chairs into circle and remind ourselves
of the following:

The Fundamental Principles of Circle

Confidentiality
Anything which we hear in circle is confidential. Even if some
trauma has been mentioned in circle and you see the woman
later in other circumstances, leave it to her to introduce the
subject if she wants to. Likewise, even within the circle we need
to be very sensitive.

Listening
We all know the difference between hearing and listening but
in circle we go one stage further to what has been called 'Rapt
listening'. This means that we listen with unconditional love,
open to be changed ourselves by what we hear: no judgement,
no interruptions, no advice, no thinking about what we are
going to say next - simply total focus on listening to the one
who is speaking.

Sarita Chawla[4] describes it as 'listening with my whole being'.
She points out:

> . . . *that it is inherently risky - the risk being that of being changed*
> *by it. It involves suspension of perceived notions, of a willingness to*
> *see the world and oneself anew and to listen with a 'beginners*

mind'. Stories of great truth and imagination are revealed, many inner questions resolve and compassion expands. There is space also to listen to one's own voice and assumptions. In some ways this may be the most significant part of listening. Unless we can deeply listen to the frames from which we speak, the vistas which we see are only part of the landscape.

Equality

Each person in the circle is of equal value and all need to be heard. A 'talking stick' is sometimes used for this. Rather than a stick we have sometimes used a shell or other small object. The person who is holding the 'talking stick' is the only one who may speak. Very often it is placed in the centre when you have finished saying what is in your heart, but usually it is a good idea to make sure that it has been right round the circle first. On the other hand, many circles dispense with this and speak either in turn or as they feel moved to contribute.

Sacred quality / transforming power

Those who have worked with the 'Twelve Step' programme for alcoholics or with the 'Alternatives to Violence project' know that there is some indefinable element involved in a group who are sharing from the heart. It may be simply the fact that when, for example, six people meet together, three and three make more than six. Whatever it is, we need to be aware. In many situations people will speak of a group 'gelling'. This is often just considered to be a matter of chance and indeed it does depend to some extent on a certain combination of personalities. However, fundamentally, it emerges from a willingness to share our vulnerability and be prepared to trust one another. This is the growth of love. To a greater or lesser extent it develops in most of our circles at the Grange. In such situations amazing things can happen. Sometimes we may wish to have a moment's silence before speaking while we tune in to this, rather than starting to speak as soon as the talking stick is in our hand.

Be aware that if one or two people tend to talk for too long it may be necessary to agree on *a time limit* for each person but usually it flows without the need for this and the aim should be to give each person as long as they need.

Process of Circle

This section relates to what we do at the Grange. It may not be appropriate for reading groups.

Opening ritual
We are undertaking a sacred task so it is good to start with an opening ritual, however simple. We always light a central candle, which at the Grange stands in a bowl of sage leaves. This not only provides a focus and reminds us that we are in session, but has resonance with ancient campfires. We dedicate the candle as we light it - perhaps to the subject which we shall be considering in the session. At the end the candle is blown out with a gesture of gratitude for all we have received.

Silence / attunement
At the Grange we have three days together and those who wish share twenty minutes' silence before breakfast each morning. Even so, it can be helpful to begin the session with a few minutes' silence while we attune to each other and to 'the spirit of wisdom' after the candle has been lit.

Rain-check
We then invite each person in turn to tell us how they feel today: 'I didn't sleep very well last night so I'm feeling tired' - 'I'm thinking about my sister's cancer'. One way or another, we tell the circle what is on our mind and how we feel.

Theme

After this we may start considering the theme for the session. This is not a discussion. Each person speaks from her heart and listens to the other person from her heart. To begin with you will need to take a familiar and 'easy' theme. A question can be a good starting point. Susan Langer[5] advises discovery of the right question because 'every answer is concealed in the question that elicited it'. At the end of the chapters on 'Authenticity' and 'Spirituality' there are some themes that could be considered while trust, love and confidence are growing. We approach the session with no results in mind. We simply encourage the spirit of enquiry and empathy in each of those taking part.

When it feels appropriate, you will want to share your stories. I have implied by the format of this book, that such life stories can only be shared when a deep level of trust has been cultivated. However, we can share on different levels and it may be that a preliminary sharing, even if on a somewhat superficial level, may be a good introductory theme. Each time we share, we may discover some other facet or forgotten depth which has come to consciousness, perhaps triggered by another story.

However, if it is to be a meaningful session, I suggest that it is only when you are all confident that love and trust are strong that you tackle 'Love', the subject of the most important chapter in this book.

Convener

Although all in the circle are equal, from a practical point of view it is helpful to have a *Convener* - a role which can be rotated - a different person for each meeting. The Convener will remind people when it is time to start and finish, will light the candle, blow it out with gratitude at the end and perhaps decide whether a 'talking stick' is appropriate.

Guardian / Grandmother

Beyond the Convener, it can also be helpful to have a *Guardian* to provide continuity and any necessary back-up between meetings. Occasionally someone will be distressed. This is natural, and to be expected. A circle can allow an unbottling of previously restrained emotions and this is healthy. Being a women's circle, there will naturally be comfort and support from the group. However, the wound may be more than can be healed in the time available and the Guardian can, indeed *must*, ensure that there is some ongoing help and support available.

At the Grange, Meg, a skilled counsellor, comes in to meet everyone for a meal on the first night and is then available for a free counselling hour on Friday or Saturday afternoon if there is a need. This provides an opportunity for following up any such issue in a one to one session. We are fortunate to have a skilled counsellor but this is not essential, as long as the group undertakes to support anyone that needs it.

Awareness of Wider Significance

The circle is a tool whereby we can discover wisdom. It may also be considered as a nest which will incubate eggs - creative new beginnings.

Jean Shinoda Bolen in her prophetic book *The Millionth Circle* foretells that when the number of women's circles have reached a critical point, there will be a shift in consciousness and a whole new way of being will emerge.

We need to be aware that our circle is one of many thousands circling the Earth and as we pursue our own truth towards wisdom we *shall* be able to change the world.

Sometimes a circle may evolve into the kind of resource group which I describe in the chapter on Spirituality.

3

AUTHENTICITY

When the heart weeps for what it has lost.
The Spirit laughs for what it has found.
Sufi saying

Our deepest fear
is not that we are inadequate.
Our deepest fear
is that we are powerful beyond measure.
It is our light, not our darkness
that most frightens us.
We ask ourselves, 'who am I
to be brilliant, gorgeous, talented, fabulous?'
Actually, who are you not to be?

You are a child of God.
Your playing small does not serve the world.
There is nothing enlightened about shrinking
so that other people won't feel insecure around you.
We are all meant to shine as children do.
We were born to make manifest
the glory of God within us.
It's not just in some of us: it's in everyone.
And as we let our own light shine,
we unconsciously give other people
permission to do the same.
As we are liberated from our own fear,
our presence automatically liberates others.
Marianne Williamson, *A Return to Love* and quoted by Nelson Mandela.

We cannot live in a world that is not our own
In a world that is interpreted for us by others.
An interpreted world is not a home.
Part of the terror is to take back our own listening.
To use our own voices. To see our own light.

Abbess Hildegard of Bingen, twelfth century mystic

Suddenly, about the time of our fiftieth birthday perhaps, we realise that we have spent half a life-time trying to live up to the expectations of parents, teachers, husbands, employers, children and now the landscape is changing and we wonder who we really are. Half a lifetime has gone, but we now have that experience under our belt so have the power to operate from the heart with our own decisions and determination. Yet, as I mentioned in the Introduction, we are so encased in assumptions about life, we may not even be aware what they are. So how do we begin to find out who we really are?

Sarita Chawla[4] suggests that a way of starting is to ask 'authentic questions'. She points out that many women have discovered that they have an atrophied 'question muscle':

We find ourselves unpractised at asking authentic questions (because as we've progressed, we've been expected to know) . . . and so we are distanced from our beginner's mind, the mind that wants to sweep out the clutter of old assumptions and to see things with a fresh perspective. As real questions often challenge our out-dated, unsurfaced assumptions, authentic questions tend to be preceded by self reflection and followed by real learning.

What it Means to be a Woman

We need to be aware that most of the definitions of woman and her mythological representation have been produced by men. We need to reassesss our assumptions and this perhaps may help men to reassess their assumptions about manhood.

One symbol of Christian culture is of the woman as a chalice, with its implication of receptive passivity - an open bowl. We may contrast this with Nut the Egyptian goddess of the sky who is an overarching semi-circle, or dome which envelops and keeps safe. The concept of the circle seems to ring true, but do we need to find the wholeness of a full circle?

Men are usually physically stronger but surely have a tender and caring component which may have been overlaid by a 'toughening-up' process, or by an inherited attitude from a more primitive past. When it is said that men need to develop their feminine side, do we mean rather that they should discover their true nature?

Women have a strength and stamina which emerges in many ways including child protection, home-making and agriculture, but above all they tend to be more emotionally articulate and prepared to explore their emotional life.

Such emotional awareness has been encouraged for girls but mostly discouraged for boys, who, perhaps with the prospect of fighting for their country and all the horrors this may entail, have been trained to 'keep a stiff upper lip' and suppress their natural emotions. This is something which now needs to be remedied.

In a world which focussed on survival, a man's role was to help provide food, construct shelter, inseminate new life and protect from harm. Today, in our western world at least, these roles are not so clearly defined. Yet the mutual love and support between men and women is still a key factor of life and extends not only into the bringing up of a family but into other areas of creativity.

Today we have the opportunity to heal the damage from the past. It is a task for both men and women, but perhaps women are more aware of the situation and able in their circles to remedy it. Men will more easily find their own true nature once women find healing themselves.

As we all contribute our life experience relating to these issues then from such diversity we shall deepen our understanding.

My own life experience is offered in the next chapters 'My Story'.

A very well known symbol from the East is the Tao image of yin and yang. Each concept has a small circle of the opposite within it and each is complementary to the other; in this respect it can represent the male-female relationship. However the usual interpretation of yin energy (woman) is 'receptive, passive and dark'. Is this symbolism helpful?

Although a woman is 'receptive' to the male seed in an act of joint creativity, it is she who gives birth in the ultimate act of creation. It is the woman who primarily nurtures the child in body and mind thus having the potential to create the next generation - the future of the world. Women are receptive in the sense of being good listeners - but they are also good communicators.

They may be described as 'passive' because they usually co-operate rather than compete - but creative co-operation is not passive. When a woman stands up to defend future generations of children (as the Greenham women did) this is described as 'cultivating her masculine side'. Not so. Protection of her young, albeit in a non-violent way, is a strong characteristic of being a woman.

Then what about darkness? Darkness contains all the colours absorbed within itself instead of just reflecting them as white light does. The darkness of the womb contains the beginnings of life; seeds germinate in darkness. To this extent perhaps a woman resembles darkness. But men and women both instinctively seek the light and often identify darkness with ignorance and evil. This is not a helpful comparison!

In the early days of psychology it was assumed that women's minds were the same as men's. But more recently such views have been challenged, not least by Jean Baker Miller's book *Towards a New Psychology of Women* in which she describes a woman's psyche as being woven from relationships. Another book published about the same time, *Knowing Woman* by Irene Claremont de Castilego, makes the distinction between men's focussed awareness and women's diffuse awareness. She blames psychologists for trying to fit people into 'normality' (*is* there such a thing?). For me these were vital seminal books because I could recognise at once the truth which they were revealing.

Medicine has traditionally been influenced by what is perceived as a male approach to illness - 'curing' by external intervention (surgical or medical). It has been suggested that the influence of women on medicine is gradually causing a shift towards involving the mind of the patient in the healing process. We surely need both approaches.

Although giving women a new freedom, feminism in its initial exuberance did much damage by proclaiming that men and women were both the same and thus encouraging women to imitate male behaviour. Women discovered that they could think and work as well as men and deserved the opportunity to do whatever they wanted to do. As Marianne Williamson points out, some serious mistakes were made and women denigrated the feminine in the name of feminism, and assumed that they were now free to behave just like men. In the name of feminism women denied some essential aspects of their authentic selves. Calling a woman 'feminine' was practically an insult, implying that a feminine woman was simply a plaything for men. Words like 'nurturing' and 'maternal' weren't viewed as feminist but as weak. If men could be tough as nails in the corporate boardroom and not factor-in the welfare of children, then so could we. If men could have sex and not get emotionally involved, then so could we. But in the last two or three generations a great correction has been underway as older women recognised that the reality of their feminine yearnings were being denied - to make a home and have a family Marianne says that she now sees that 'it is a woman's God given role to tend to the home and take care of the children; it's just that the entire planet is our home and every child on it is one of our children. And that would change the world.'

Women need to be out in the world if that's where they feel led to be, but not at the expense of their spiritual mission: 'to proclaim that the world is our home and we're responsible for all its children.' She continues, 'Women should be the keepers of the conscience of the world . . . keepers of the internal flame - the light of humanitarian values and the primacy of love - and our greatest power lies in keeping it lit.'

Women's increasing independence (which is often based on hurts from the past), and the cultural lens through which many men see women simply as sex objects, does not help to heal this distortion and is yet another reason why we need to understand more about love and include men in our exploration.

Today we have the opportunity to heal the damage from the past. It is a task for both men and women, but perhaps women are more aware of the situation and able, in their circles, to remedy it. Men will more easily find their own true nature once women find healing themselves.

Age

We are no longer young. Let's celebrate our maturity. The years after the menopause can be the opportunity to put our energies into what we care most about. Either work or childcare have probably taken all our energies for the last twenty years or so, but now there needs to be some other prime focus in our lives. It is a time to explore areas for which there has been no opportunity up to now; to develop talents which have been latent or undiscovered.

We realised that unlike some cultures, there is no recognised role for older women in our society. Yet Jung thought that it had a significance which needs to be explored. Of course it may be too facile to speak of 'a role' when we are all so different but it seems that there is some positive contribution which we could all make in our different ways. Why ignore the value of so many years of life experience? Some may not wish to make a contribution at all.

There may be identifiable roles which an older woman may

play such as a healer, mediator, cook, gardener, musician. Many of us are able to teach some of the old crafts such as knitting, spinning and crochet which were in danger of dying out. Those who were children during the war may also have much to teach about economy which is relevant to our new ecological awareness.

For many, however, this period is haunted by the fear of disability and old age. Many of the images in the media portray older people as having lost their mental as well as their physical abilities. Sadly some may suffer from Alzheimer's or dementia in later years but most not only retain their judgement and mental acumen but have the added quality of wisdom.

What happens to our brains as we get older? Many people assume that mental and physical abilities necessarily decline with age; that we are, after age twenty-five, losing significant brain capacity on a daily basis. In fact, Michael Gelb[7] says that the average brain can improve with age. Our neurones are capable of making increasingly complex new connections throughout our lives. And our neuronal endowment is so great that, even if we lost a thousand brain cells every day for the rest of our lives, it would still be 'less than 1 per cent of our total' (of course it's important not to lose the 1 per cent that we actually use!). Perhaps we too readily identify moments of memory lapse as 'senior moments' when in fact we can observe this happening among younger age groups as well.

Professor Greenfield[8] said, 'I'm constantly surprised at the amazing way the brain can adapt. I believe it's one of the very few parts of our bodies that really does get better with age. While everything else begins to sag and slip, the brain just becomes more individual as time goes on.' Dr Francine Benes[9] from Harvard Medical School has recently discovered that around the age of fifty there is a significant growth in myelin, the fatty coating to nerve fibres that insulates and speeds up connection between nerve cells. This helps us synthesise our experience and enables us to make wiser decisions.

Some women, grieving for their lost youth and changed looks, sometimes take radical measures to try and restore face and figure, with an aim to extend their sexual attraction. But sexual attraction does not depend entirely on these. Betty Frieden[10] in her book *The Fount of Age* speaks of, 'An intimacy beyond the dreams of youth' - and it is surely this that we should value, whether or not it has any physical manifestation.

The period between the menopause and old age is a time of 'maturity', a significant and vital part of life. This probably coincides with the years between fifty to seventy but will obviously vary and for many the period will extend much longer. In the first years after the menopause the body settles down into a new rhythm. There may not be the vitality and energy of earlier years (although I know from my own experience that there can be) but it is a time of new directions and for renewed consideration of life values in preparation for the growing wisdom which may come with later years. We have only to look at some of the women in public life, and older women we may know personally, who continue to make a significant contribution to the community well into their seventies and beyond. This is a relatively new phenomenon, having emerged during the last fifty years and is not yet widely recognised, especially as it has coincided with the burgeoning of the cult of youth. In finding our authenticity we need to affirm and rejoice in the age we are, instead of holding on to a youth which has gone. We now have a new freedom and the opportunity to 'make a difference'.

Our Roots

Clearly we owe something of our personality to our genes. Occasionally we may be able to find out something about where our forebears lived and who they were, but observation of a few recent ancestors can be misleading, especially when it comes to inherited characteristics.

For all our searching, few of us can trace our lineage back for more than a few generations. In the context of the thousands and thousands of years in our history we are wonderfully inter-related. It was once the custom to follow back the male line in the family tree as if this represented the only root, and admittedly this was easier with our Western custom of taking the male name in marriage. However, I have two parents, four grandparents, sixteen great grandparents and so on. Take this back and by the time we get to 1600 I have more than 18,000 ancestors, by 1400 more than a million. By the time of the Norman Conquest the figure is probably larger than the entire population of this island.

Clearly some of our ancestors must have appeared more than once but I find it quite wonderful and humbling to realise how many people were involved in my creation and to how many I must now be related. My genetic heritage is not a fixed blue-print but an amazing kaleidoscope of potential which I have hardly begun to tap into. And of course this is something which I share with those who were adopted and may not be able to trace their natural parents.

However, having said that, it can be helpful to look at the ancestors we know of, including our parents, and consider whether they would say they had lived happy and fulfilling lives. And if so why? Did they 'make a difference'? - to those around them? - to the wider world? - to their descendants including ourselves? Are there any whom we would wish to emulate?

Names

Do you like your name? Names are important in that they colour our perception of ourselves. Do you know what your name means? If you don't like it, would you like to change it and, if so, what other name would you choose? Several women who have come to our weekends, who have not liked their names, have tried a new one for the weekend and sometimes stayed with it afterwards.

Relationships

One of the ways we define who we are, as Jean Baker Miller pointed out, is through our relationships. We identify ourselves as 'the wife of . . .', 'the daughter of . . . ' , 'the friend of . . . ', 'the sister of . . . ', 'the mother of . . .' A recent survey has discovered that at times of tension women resort to female company whereas a man will go away and hole up by himself. Maintaining a healthy psyche involves maintaining good relationships and it is through relationships that growth can come. Yet at mid-life all sorts of changes may be happening in these relationships: children may be leaving home, or at least becoming more independent; we may be retiring from a job which we have really enjoyed (or hated) and losing the companionship of work colleagues; husbands/partners may be retiring; parents may be becoming more dependent and friends moving away. All these relationships need adjustment and can contain the possibility of enrichment in the process. They are all also potential sources of hugs. It is said that good health requires four hugs a day and it must surely be significant that hugging also promotes relationship with another person.

Friendship
In the context of the second half of life I put 'friendship' at the top of my list. Apart from single women who already know the value of friendship there will be widows and divorcees at this stage of life for whom friendship will take on a new priority.

Old friends are good friends because they share so many memories and know so much about who we are, but they often move away. At the same time there will be the opportunity for new friends. Ruth aged eighty-nine said that the last fifteen years had been the most healthy in her life and one of the reasons for this was that she had now five good friends whereas earlier she had not had the opportunity to make friends as she had been so occupied with work and caring. We need to be open to the enrichment of such new friends (of all ages, both men and women) and not confine ourselves in a tight circle of 'the known'. In our twenties and thirties our friends may have been the parents of our children's friends or our work colleagues. It may be only in maturity that we can discover friends who are truly on the same wavelength and share interests which we now have the opportunity to develop. Moving now to the network of relationships within the family:

Marriage

'I am dreading my husband's retirement. He just wants to sit and put his feet up or play a round of golf and wants me to be with him all the time. But I have now found freedom and started opening doors to all sorts of new interests.' How often we hear this cry or something similar. Yet there are no longer the constrictions of coping with the traumas of adolescent children or the stresses of work, so there is opportunity for getting to know one another on a deeper level while developing new centres of focus and interest.

The awakening experience of a woman who has embarked on a course of education or training may feel quite threatening to a partner unless he can be in some way included in the experience. Some women, at our weekends, observed that roles at this period are often reversed. Whereas the wife played a supporting role during her husband's working life, it is often he who now can do the same for her. In the modern household of two careers the house-husband may already have assumed this pattern. In the past our marriage vows to 'love each other until death do us part' usually envisaged a much shorter length of time than today. In many ways we are not the same people at fifty as we were at twenty. Often children of another marriage are involved in the equation. Occasionally there may even be a change in sexual orientation. Marriage can be a most enriching growth experience but there surely needs to be a reassessment at mid-life.

Christina Baldwin suggests in her book *Calling the Circle* that the circle technique can helpfully be applied to marriage adaptation. One partner speaks from the heart while the other listens, without interruption, judgement or advice. Then the roles are reversed. And so on. (Someone pointed out that you cannot expect from a person what they are perhaps not capable of giving.) A consideration of how time and money are to be spent can lead on to a consideration of priorities and from there possibly to the whole meaning of life, or at least to ensuring that each can follow their own path within the relationship. It can be worth thinking about how much we may confuse 'loyalty' with 'possessiveness'. We also need to scotch the myth that a happy marriage depends on 'being in love'. Many of the happiest marriages have been arranged by parents on the basis of shared values and compatibility. It is up to us to generate the dynamics which make a marriage work and as we enter the second half of life we probably need a deliberate adaptation. Susan Page[11] suggests, 'if even only one partner learns how to love openly and freely, aware of the spiritual level, then the relationship can be transformed.'

If the marriage does end, there needs to be an awareness of the potential loneliness of one or both partners, who may feel deprived not only of the partner's companionship but also of the whole complex of their partner's family. Such links can often be maintained amicably.

Children

Another major changing relationship is that of parent and child. The child moves from dependence on the parent to growing independence and friendship. As parents we need to acknowledge this and have the courage to let go. John Russel's poem expresses this very well:

> *I don't want to go, but it started*
> *At the moment of my birth, my departure.*
> *It was arrival and departure*

And you had to finish what you started,
You let me go.
I didn't want to go this way,
Remembering your pride at those first steps
Taken in the right direction, but then
You took the hardest step, and left me free
To make my own selection, you let me go.

I didn't want to leave you yet
I really wasn't ready
But you never held me back
And you showed through love and kindness
No matter how far I get
There's always something binds us.

I didn't want to go this far
To where I cannot hold you;
But now this path's been started
Send me on my way with the love
That's never going to part us
And let me go.

As a child grows into maturity a relationship can deepen although adjustment will be needed including taking account of their new friends and relationships. The situation becomes even more complex when the son or daughter is still living at home in their twenties or even thirties.

Grandmothering is a recognised role which in many cases has now become more difficult because of the way families have broken up or live at a distance. But for the same reason, many older women who have no grandchildren of their own can take on the role of mentor. This may involve simply listening, asking key questions, befriending, affirming and encouraging. It can also mean bringing a sense of perspective and possibly suggesting new horizons. Detta had lived with the Hopi Indians and she told us that in their culture the grandmothers observe the young and identify any latent talents which can then be encouraged. We may not be very clever in learning about some of the new technology, but experience of how we coped with failure, broken relationships or bereavement can still be very relevant.

In a society haunted by fears of sexual abuse, it may be that older women can be some of the few people able to hug and cuddle children to give reassurance and comfort. Many of us resonate with Diana Looman's well known poem:

> *If I had my child to raise again*
> *I'd fingerpaint more and point the finger less*
> *I'd do less correcting and more connecting . . .*
> *I'd teach less about the love of power*
> *and more about the power of love*

As grandmothers we have a second chance, especially as we may then be operating in a lower gear which is more compatible with childhood.

The Hopi Indians have a saying that 'When the grandmothers speak, the earth will be saved.'

Older women used to be revered in many cultures as holding the memory and providing stability in a link between generations. The preservation of old values is something we need to look at, but we need to evaluate what we are preserving. Such values can be passed on through the traditional art of storytelling. Many of our old children's stories send 'the wrong message' today. Already feminist groups have rewritten some of our stories so that the ultimate aim of a young girl is not to marry her prince and live happily ever after.

However, there are other stories which need to be reviewed and perhaps rewritten.

One of these stories is 'St George and the dragon'. In China a dragon is a humorous creature full of fun. Why do we in the West perceive him as fearful and dangerous? Unfortunately the message it gives to children is that if they see anything which seems bad or evil they should attack it and kill it. They might have a wrong perception. I like the new story much better which also replaces conflict by transformation and is the one I tell my grandchildren.

In this story when the dragon starts killing the villagers and the king is looking round for a virgin to sacrifice, the queen says, "Calm down now. I expect he's just hungry!" and she gathers her ladies around her. She also calls St George away from polishing up his halo and invites him to come and help her. Between them they all make an enormous cake which George courageously takes down to the forest. The dragon appears and looks at it suspiciously. Then he tries it . . . and really enjoys it. "Yum! Yum!" So they repeat the cake every few days and gradually the dragon begins to help them light their fires, pull their timber wagons and give them free transport by air to the neighbouring countries. Meanwhile George becomes an expert chef and his 'dragon breath curries' are renowned throughout the land.

Many other stories could be rewritten in this way.

Parents

For many embarking on the second half of life their own parents are still around and may need varying degrees of care and time. This may be an opportunity to get to know a parent as never before and to encourage them to tell the story of their own lives. But many are faced with parents who are beyond this and mainly in need of physical care and support.

This can be an exhausting situation both emotionally and physically and we need to realise that almost certainly we need additional help. This may not be easy to come by but it is worth persevering and making it a priority. Apart from anything else, an exhausted person does not make a good carer. Sometimes a group of friends can ease this responsibility in rotation. (This is where the resource groups explored in a later chapter, p.103, would have relevance.)

Siblings

Another relationship which has often been considered in our exploration is that of a sibling. Several women spoke of brothers or sisters who were once close but had grown apart during the years and some now wanted to restore the relationship. There was also the person in a long-standing unhappy relationship wanting to make a reconciliation with her sister. This type of situation may hinge on the relationship which each had with a parent, living or dead which may involve a whole complex of healing.

In these days of the internet and increasing accessibility of family records, illegitimate siblings may trace their lineage and appear to a family for the first time. This presents a new situation, bringing all sorts of ghosts from the past, and new relationships needing to be created.

This section on relationships is very relevant to one of the main themes of this book - the idea that we need to focus on the energies which operate *between* us.

Freedom

Sometimes the reaction to emerging from the restrictions of home and employment can be similar to that of the adolescent emerging from school. One woman said that she missed out on adolescent rebellion because she was looking after younger siblings and she now has a wild desire to have a tattoo and a passionate love affair . . . a wild urge to kick over the traces and do all the things she could never do before - as in Jenny Joseph's warning:

When I am an old woman I shall wear purple
With a red hat which doesn't go and doesn't suit me.
And I shall spend my pension on brandy and summer gloves
And satin sandals, and say we've no money for butter

I shall sit down on the pavement when I'm tired
And gobble up samples in shops and press alarm bells.
And run my stick along the railings
And make up for the sobriety of my youth.

. . . in fact, growing old disgracefully. It can be fun and exhilarating. On the other hand this form of escapism can too easily degenerate into an ongoing way of life which simply provides fuel for those who see old age as a source of merriment ('What's grandma up to now?') and a liability. And is it really authentic?

Wouldn't it be true to say that it is only when we can move from this reactive behaviour to a way of living which springs from the heart centre that we shall find true freedom and significance in our life?

Occupation

One of the other elements that define who we are in our society is our occupation. So at a time of retirement or with the family leaving home there may be a sense of being cast adrift. Yet for many it is an opportunity to take a new direction and to use energy in discovering long buried creativity, or in a way which is more in line with our deepest concerns.

'What do you do?' people ask. Probably many women these days can reply, 'Doctor, nurse, journalist, banker, consultant, teacher,farmer, nursery gardener, receptionist' etc. Impressive - but zap! you have immediately been pigeonholed. For those who didn't work, by choice or by necessity, the response in the past was all too often, 'I'm only a housewife' instead of setting forth the enormous variety of skills involved in this task - skills that are now increasingly being recognised: baby and child-care expert, teacher, cook, nurse, caterer, household manager, accountant, painter and decorator, etc, etc. Many of us too readily underestimate our skills.

However, it is true that such housebound work lacks intellectual stimulus and it is often those who have been most confined to the home who are hungry at middle-age for some intellectual stretching. One of the women who came on our weekends drew her life up to fifty as a woman with her eyes closed. Then, as she began to study, her eyes opened, and a whole new world was revealed.

Some who do not want to embark on the discipline of a university course find mental stimulation in the classes of the University of the Third Age[12]. This idea was started in France in 1972 and encourages people over the age of fifty to enjoy learning and leisure interests, to make new friends and to help each other. Members are not students and qualifications are neither required nor given. There are no paid tutors but members with some special skill or area of knowledge share this with others who wish to learn. It is very friendly and relaxed and there are now branches of the University in most British towns.

Before making any decisions about training or making long-term commitments, we need to know in which direction we want to go. What do we care about most? Many women take a course in counselling at this point in their lives, and this may also be a good basis for other training. A course in creative writing may lead to journalling (keeping a diary) which itself enriches life and can throw up pointers to the next stage. It is also helpful to give some time to exploring possibilities and finding out what is involved, perhaps getting experience on a temporary basis as you decide what it is you want to do most. This may take two years or more and is sometimes called the 'Fertile Void'. It is not an easy place to be as it lacks signposts and familiar surroundings, yet it may enable us to make the most creative use of the years ahead and it is here that friendships can be especially valuable. The shared exploration of the 'Second Half of Life' weekends can be part of this search and can help to focus the way forward.

It might at this point be worth saying a word about voluntary work. Our modern society would probably collapse if it were not for the large number of voluntary workers, yet they are not adequately valued. They are often considered to be 'untrained', which is far from the truth as many voluntary workers today have both experience and skills. Our materialist society often asserts that we don't value anything unless we pay for it and many in the second half of life might indeed prefer to be able to supplement their pension with paid work. However, many others want to give back with gratitude for what they have been given and voluntary work in response to some need can be a way of doing this.

Future path

This period between retirement and discovering a new way of life can be an uncomfortable, disorienting time but can be given focus by asking such questions as:

What makes my heart sing? What make me feel fully alive? These include experiences which are energising and filled with wonder. Walking by the sea or on the mountains? Dancing barefoot on the grass? Singing in a choir? Hearing the laughter of children? Being in love? Listening to bird-song? Talking with a friend about things which matter? Being able to help or affirm someone else? Often there is awareness of a bigger universe, of unity, meaning, of love and beauty. (It is revealing to discover, too, how many of the items which are usually listed do not depend on physical agility or wealth and are equally available to the aged and less mobile.)

What are the issues in life which I care about most? Saving the environment? Creating peace? Searching for some way of giving hope to the young homeless? Land-mine clearance? The rehabilitation of prisoners? Developing painting skills? Writing a book?
What are the skills I already have and what new skills would I like to develop? Cooking? Listening? Organising? Writing? Playing with children?

What do I really enjoy doing? Reading? Walking? Painting? Talking to friends? Meeting challenges? This can be expanded into favourite foods, places, books, music, etc.

What are the achievements in my life? Perhaps surviving an ordeal? Coping with failure or illness? Going on a pilgrimage? Being one of a team who laid on some event? Starting a new business or other project? Writing a poem? Playing a musical instrument?

It is worth taking time to reflect on these things because so often we discount them and they lie in a mental waste-paper basket when they could be providing fuel for lighting fires. (Phoenix fires, not fires of demolition!!)

One thing which underpins everything else is to keep mentally and physically agile through a healthy life-style.

Story of Your Life

Wisdom is based on our life experience. We may draw on the life experience of those who have lived before us, but we need to remember that they, too, were only human beings like ourselves who were also looking for the meaning of life. Some may have been wiser than others, as some people today may be wiser than others, but the fact that they lived a long time ago and in more limited times does not give their thoughts any extra special value. Do not undervalue your own life experience.

It can be a good rite of passage at mid-life to write the story of your life so far. and it can then be even more affirming and enriching to share it with a friend or in circle as we often resonate with the experiences of others or see new significance in some of the events of our own lives This can sharpen our focus on who we are and where we are going.

Women have been sitting in groups or circles telling their stories since time began, but sometimes in our modern life women become unused to all-female company and are surprised at how sympathetic and supportive this can be. In our groups we have felt free to talk about things which we have never talked about before, from the physical to the spiritual. Hearing our own story can bring about change. There is no possibility of telling all the events in our lives, so inevitably we need to be selective. Thinking about it afterwards, we can reflect on why it was that we chose the events we did. Sometimes it could have been an empathic echo of someone else's story; sometimes we may have omitted an event which was of vital significance. Why? We can also approach our life stories on different levels and if this is the first time you have done this, you may find that later on, as the trust within the circle increases, it is possible to make contact with deeper levels of experience.

Another way of approaching this, and to tap into the intuitive right brain, is to draw your *Tree of Life*. Give yourself plenty of time (an hour at least), a really large sheet of paper and some coloured pencils or paints. Your project is to draw the tree of your own life. You do not need to be an artist or even good at drawing - in fact it may be an advantage if you are not, because you will not be distracted into trying to present an attractive finished picture. It is astonishing how different each tree can be and how each has its own individual beauty. This will enable you to see the shape of your life and to identify skills and dreams which may have been buried or repressed but which can now have an opportunity to bear fruit.

In our exploration groups we find it helpful to do a standing meditation before we start:

Imagine that we are trees in a grove . . . just close enough to give each other support and yet far enough apart to give room for growth.

Imagine the roots of your tree going back into the past. Remember the emotional and spiritual roots and the people in your childhood and youth who gave you love and hope and encouragement and helped to make you who you are.

Your roots were nurtured by the sunshine - good times of joy, love, affirmation, and achievement, but also by the compost of the hard times, the grief, the pain, rejection, ending a relationship, failing an exam, losing a job.

Such compost may need to be worked through but it contains rich nourishment for growth and for healing others. This is what is meant by the wounded healer.

So be aware of this, but do not spend too long on the past now.

Move up the trunk of the tree to the branches reaching upwards to the sky.

Your tree has grown beyond the first flowering and the potential of physical fruit, but there is now the prospect of spiritual and emotional fruit and you can imagine these in any way you wish among the upper branches. They will connect very much with the issues which you are concerned about, your dreams, your skills, the potential which you may wish to explore, qualities you wish to develop, new interests, a new attitude to life or the maturing of a long held vision.

Your tree has stood for many years through the winds and snows of winter, through the sunshine and rain of spring and summers. It is descended from trees going right back to the beginning of the world, each one individual and beautiful in its own way and with fruit to offer to the world, and seeds which may only take root and grow in a future after you are gone. Now, holding this image in your mind, allow it to emerge again when you sit down to draw.

When we draw our Trees of Life at the Grange we allot about an hour to the exercise. Some people feel they have finished in less than that time, but it is usually worth sitting for a while with it and being open to anything else which comes to mind. Some people want to go on adding bits for a long time afterwards, but after an hour there will usually be enough to share in a small group. From such an exercise we can move a long way forward towards authenticity and many people say afterwards that this is the most helpful part of the weekend.

THEMES FOR GROUP SHARING - A SUMMARY

1. Do you like your name?

2. Are you glad you are a woman? / man?

3. What makes your heart sing? What makes you feel fully alive?

4. a) Think of some achievements and what effect these have had on your life.
   b) Think of some failures. How did you cope?

5. How do you feel about the second half of life?

6. Have you had a life changing experience?

7. Who are the people you most admire?

8. Name one thing (such as education, homelessness, conservation, etc.) which you care about passionately and to which you might be in a position to make a difference. (Beware that this does not degenerate into a whinge about lack of action from the government!)

9. What are the driving forces in your life?

10. Draw the Tree of your Life and bring it to the session to share.

4

My Story - Part One

We shall not cease from exploration
And the end of all our exploring
Will be to arrive where we started
And know the place for the first time.
Through the unknown, remembered gate
When the last of earth left to discover
Is that which was the beginning;
At the source of the longest river
The voice of the hidden waterfall
And the children in the apple tree
Not known, because not looked for
But heard, half-heard, in the stillness
Between two waves of the sea.
Quick now, here now, always -
A condition of complete simplicity
(Costing not less than everything)

from *Little Gidding* by T. S. Eliot

Come down O Love divine.
Seek Thou this soul of mine
And visit it with Thine own ardour glowing

Charles Wesley

For you there is only one road that can lead to God and that is
fidelity to remain constantly true to yourself to what you feel is
highest in you.
The road will open before you as you go.

Teilhard de Chardin

It may seem strange to insert the story of my life in the middle of a book like this. However, I have invited you to share your stories and as I mentioned before, it is only from life experience that we can draw wisdom. The contents of this book have grown from my life experience and it will enable the reader to understand the remainder of the book more fully.

An underlying thread in my whole life has been my search for the truth about love. When I was about fifty I wondered if I had discovered a new aspect of this. It is only now after thirty years that I feel sufficiently confident to be able to write about it, and see the meaning in it. I hope my story will be revealing and will find resonance in the reader. This is by no means my whole story. Who could tell that? But I have selected the events which have bearing on my search for the truth about love and later my interest in 'peak experience' and spirituality. I have divided my life into two parts. Part One up to the age of fifty and Part Two from that time up to the present.

Early Days

From the perspective of later years, I am very grateful to have been born into a Methodist family. This meant that although we did not have very much money, my parents and both sets of grandparents were teetotal and would not gamble even on a church raffle. From its beginnings, Methodism[13] was concerned with social problems so our family had an awareness, inherited from previous generations, of the damage and misery which addictions to such things as alcohol and gambling could bring.

This may sound very austere and drab but it was far from that; there was plenty of laughter and song. There was a natural enthusiasm for life, an interest in learning more about the world and, in true Methodist spirit, a love of music, especially singing together.

We were fortunate, too, that for many generations our family had been spared the ravages of war.

We were not physically demonstrative - none of the hugs and cuddles of today - but our love for each other, although not always immediately obvious, was assumed to be there and was real. We were very well cared for and felt valued, knowing that we could rely for support not only on our immediate family but on an extended range of uncles, aunts and cousins. All this laid the foundation for a very loving, secure and happy childhood.

I was brought up in a family of three sisters. My mother, who was also one of three sisters, had been to university. Maybe it was because of this that it never even crossed my mind, until I encountered such ideas in my late teens, that anyone should consider men and women unequal. I had a matriarchal grandmother and proactive aunts and, in my perception, women played an equal and complementary role in family and community affairs. It seemed natural that men and women should work in partnership, so Feminism never became a great issue for me, although I give wholehearted support to those who are struggling for justice and equality.

We all went to church every Sunday morning and to Sunday school in the afternoon. Perhaps it was as a result of this that I felt from an early age that I had a vocation to serve God - a vocation that I expected would mean giving up any idea of marriage and devoting my life to doing some kind of work among the poor and oppressed. On the other hand this may have resulted from my grandmother's hopes for my father being projected on to me. It may have been because at a very young age I misunderstood my mother's explanation of 'the facts of life' and thought that I could never have any children. Or it may even have been that my mother gave me the idea: she had never used her university degree and perhaps, feeling that her own life had been a failure, she hoped that I would fulfil what she had missed. Be that as it may, I felt I had a special vocation.

I was in hospital a number of times as a child and was inspired by some of the nurses who looked after me and especially by a film called *The Lamp Still Burns* about the dedication of a nurse. I very much wanted to be a nurse myself but my mother insisted that my health would never be good enough.

I had little knowledge of sex in my youth, nor felt that I needed it - life was so full with books, music (I played the violin), bird-watching, sketching, cycling and boating that there was little time to think of anything else. Sex was something which happened to create babies inside marriage and our extended family gave me no cause to think otherwise. I knew nothing about contraception until I was about to get married.

My parents gave us plenty of freedom assuming that, on the basis of a good grounding, we would, in return, be sensible and considerate - which on the whole we were.

My father, having read Greats (Classics) at Oxford and extended his repertoire into physical education, was headmaster of a boys' junior school. He was also a Methodist lay preacher and a scout master. I learnt, subconsciously, the dynamics of the campfire circle at an early age.

When I was about twelve or thirteen, my father gave me a book called *The Spirit* which was a collection of essays and included a chapter about Time. I was immediately fascinated. My cousin David and I read all we could about the subject (although there wasn't much available) and thought about it and discussed it on our bird-watching expeditions in the Lake District (where our family was fortunate enough to spend all the war years). The riddle of chronological time and eternity has always intuitively seemed to be of key importance - a concept beyond our present understanding, yet possibly the gateway to a new dimension

We belonged to a Bible-reading fellowship in which selected passages from the Bible, with commentary, were decreed for every day. However, in my teens I decided to read the whole Bible right through. I did this with a mixture of boredom, shock and horror, as well as finding depth and beauty in some of the more familiar texts. I asked who wrote the Bible and realised that it had not been written by God but was in fact written by human beings like ourselves who were divinely inspired. Some (small parts) seemed to have eternal significance but other sections appeared to have a relevance primarily for the time in which they were written.

For me the most vital part lay in the gospels of the New Testament which tells the life story and teachings of Jesus Christ (no doubt interpreted through the mind-set of their time by the men who recorded it all). Christ has remained an inspiration down the ages. These books are followed by the lives, teachings and prophecy of his followers. But then the Bible suddenly stops about two thousand years ago with a curse on anyone who should add anything more. Has no one been divinely inspired since then? It seemed fairly obvious to me, even in my youth, that there had been much inspired writing in the Christian tradition by such people as Hildegard of Bingen, George Fox, Julian of Norwich, John Wesley to name but a very few. The Jews were probably ahead of their time in many ways, which is no doubt why it was their culture which gave birth to Jesus, and why their ancient scriptures were so uncritically revered. But I was not an Israeli. This was not my family history. And times have moved on.

I have said that we were a church-going family and we often discussed the sermon, even at quite a young age. I knew that the whole essence of Christ's message was that we should love one another. But what did we mean by 'love'? I could feel it in the family, especially when we gathered round the piano on a Sunday evening and my grandmother played and we would all sing her favourite hymn '*Yes God is good*', but although the people at church were, on the whole, friendly this did not seem to me to be quite what Christ had in mind. The family had an open-minded but very intellectual approach to Christianity which led to long and lively discussions over the dinner table but did not help when it came to 'love'. The Church seemed to have so many rules and regulations for channelling love in what were considered to be the 'right' way. We were told to 'love one another', but I knew I could not love someone like Mrs B. who was always putting people down and taking offence for no reason. Maybe I would have gone to her rescue in an emergency, but this was surely not enough. I realised that I could try to understand her better and this might help - but not much. I heard so many clergymen saying, 'I don't like her but of course I love her!' which I found totally incomprehensible. I supposed it meant a kind of woolly well-wishing - but I couldn't believe that that was what Christ really meant.

I also knew that there were people who were just overflowing with love and laughter, but this did not seem to be because of anything they had learnt in church. With hindsight I suspect that they came from generations of loving parents.

Then, when I was twelve, I fell in love. He was a boy called Francis, whom I hardly knew, but he passed under the window of our house every evening and it was a priority to be there in time to see him. I had vaguely puzzled about what it meant to 'fall in love' before this time and had wondered if perhaps I was in love with any of my boy cousins. However, when I actually did 'fall in love' there was no doubt. The whole world felt wonderful. What if Christ had been talking about something like this? An emotion *this* powerful! My eyes were opened for the first time to the incredible energising power of this type of love.

I discovered soon after that 'the light of my life' had a girlfriend in the village but although I felt slightly jealous I also felt that this was a good thing, a sacrifice I must make, because I could keep him on the back-burner and stay in love with him for the rest of my life. Then I would never fall in love again with anyone who might want to get married. This seemed to fit perfectly with my life plan; after all, I had a vocation!

So much for plans! When I was sixteen I went to a summer music school and fell hopelessly in love again - with a cellist whom I will call James - and Francis was forgotten. We did not get to know each other well enough to keep in touch and so I still felt comfortable with the situation - he would replace Francis on the back-burner and remain there as a safeguard against any other possibly more detrimental contender (detrimental to my vocation, that is).

However life did not for long remain so clear cut. In my last year at school I was working for an exam in English literature covering especially the 'Romantic poets'. A new teacher arrived who brought exciting new insights into what we were studying. I had always loved poetry but Jill pointed out that these writers and poets were looking for meaning in life, as we were ourselves, and her enthusiasm for what we were studying took me to new heights of emotional awareness. I fell deeply in love with her. It was a joyous gratitude for her existence and for our shared interest in literature. There was no physical attraction. I did not see her as a role model, nor was my love possessive. Indeed I secretly planned that she might marry a friend of mine whom she had never even met, but whom I thought would make an ideal match. This love coexisted with my love for James. It was equally intense but of a completely different nature.

Such teenage experiences are often dismissed simply as 'schoolgirl crushes'. It is easy to diagnose this in terms of hormone changes but the significant element was that another person was involved even if they themselves had no awareness of it. Their essence was a key component in the relationship. Those around me assumed that this had a sexual basis and as such in a girl's school was to be discouraged. However, looking back I can understand that it was something which I now call 'inspirational love'. It was enriching and a very positive and creative element in my life at that time. We need to learn a sensitivity which can identify this kind of relationship because it can be damaging to misread it. I write more about this in the chapter on 'Love'.

I had begun boarding at the age of fifteen but this was only because, in the upheavals at the end of the war, our school went in one direction and our parents went in another; in order to maintain continuity of education in a small and caring school, our parents made great financial sacrifice to enable my sister and myself to board. They each wrote to us every week and we wrote our weekly letter home. It was a discipline which I now value, as a letter can be carefully crafted and worded and often written on two levels. I have found many times in life that it has been more helpful to write a letter and give it to someone, even if they are living in the same house, rather than try and say things which may be interrupted or misunderstood.

A very memorable event happened around this time. I played the violin and used to practise in a bathroom (which anyone who sings in the bath will know has excellent acoustics). At the time, I was working for an exam on a piece of Vivaldi and had been told on no account to play it up to speed until the exam, but just to go through it slowly, carefully, and repeatedly. The top half of the large bathroom window was open to the sky and, as I played, a thunderstorm blew up. I suddenly felt 'Blow the exam!' and let rip, playing as I have never played before or since, being at one with the music and the storm. It was an unforgettable experience. I have no recollection of the exam!

During my last year at school we had a visit from Dr James Welch who was at that time head of religious broadcasting at the BBC. He also had overseas experience and his current enthusiasm was for the Groundnuts Scheme in East Africa. This was a vast project for growing groundnuts which many people thought would raise East Africa out of poverty. His interest was in helping to preserve the indigenous values of that culture against the depredations of Western society such as alcoholism, materialism and prostitution. Quite how he thought I would fit into all this I cannot imagine at this point, but at the time he convinced me that there would be a need for social workers to go out and cope with this situation and it gave me a specific objective to aim for. "Get your degree and then come back to me," he said.

As I've mentioned already, my mother had a university educa- tion and both my parents assumed that the best way they could show their love was by making sure I had the same opportunity. It is true that my grandmother, Mary Hawking, as the wife of a farmer, ruined by crop failures and animal diseases, realised that education would be the key to a much fuller life and, by setting

up a village school (where she did most of the teaching and cater-
ing herself) she enabled both my father and his brother to obtain
an Oxford education which opened new horizons for them. So
it must have seemed obvious to my father that this was the way
forward - that I must aim for Oxford.

However, the school where I was boarding, although
admirable in many ways, was not able to teach at the level of
Oxford entrance, so for the last year of education, I went to
stay with my uncle who was headmaster of a boys' school. I
have many good memories of him but one of the most valuable
lessons I learned from him was that in the search for truth I
should always rely on my own experience (advice that was later
reiterated by my tutor at university). Interestingly, when I tried
to pass this on to my son more recently he wisely said, "But my
own experience is too limited. I have to take most things on
trust." This is true, of course, but I still believe that my own
experience can be a starting point, which, through sharing with
others, can then be tested out. If I am not sure, I ask, and at
least I do not go along with saying something just because
everybody else is saying it. Truth has many facets. In later life I
realise that my quest for it was made very much smoother
because I was living in a milieu of unconditional love from the
family and extended family. Had I been lacking this, I may well
have felt the need to agree or conform in order to obtain
approval and love.

But of course my uncle was not the only person involved in
this sojourn in a boy's school. I rapidly became aware of the
adolescent male's obsession with sex, especially with extra
inside information supplied by cousins . . . Becoming aware of
this in a safe environment, I learnt how to deal with it: to be
impervious to the fantasies and innuendoes, to view them
objectively and to laugh rather than get upset . . . and later,
(especially as a Samaritan) to be compassionate when such
obsession surfaced in later life. Yet the realisation that our
society included such lusty attraction under the umbrella word
'love', in fact often assumed that this was the key meaning,

further confused my understanding of the word.

Then, at the age of seventeen, I had an experience that added yet another facet to 'love'. It happened one morning as I was walking through a wood on my way to take my Oxford entrance exam. It was a beautiful sparkling sunny morning. I saw a chaffinch perched on a branch of silver birch singing its heart out and I stopped to look and listen. And the experience became much more than the chaffinch song; it filled my whole being with an ecstasy, a sense of 'knowing' which I could not have put into words and a feeling of one-ness not only with the bird but with the whole universe. I had fleetingly had such experiences before when out in the hills of the Lake District, but this time I began to think more about it. It was a true and sacred moment, and it touched something deeper within me than any experience I'd had in church. Part of the experience was that I was filled with an energising love and this, especially, was quite unlike anything I had felt in church. In fact it was more like 'being in love'.

Oxford and After

Eventually I got to Oxford (although I am not sure that I was really Oxford material) and I thoroughly enjoyed my three years there, fully aware that it was a huge privilege.

I am especially grateful to two brilliant tutors. One was Iris Murdoch who had a passion for finding truth in a moral quagmire. Her moral philosophy related to the way we live our life today so had an immediate relevance. She was like an oasis in an arid desert of logical positivism[14]. I was very sorry to see the portrayal of her in the recent film which bears her name - it gave no conception of the inspiring tutor she had been before Alzheimer's struck. My second tutor was Peter Ady, a beautiful Burmese woman who grasped life with both hands and related the economics she was teaching to the reality of the present world.

Apart from the excitement and stimulation of new knowledge gained from my tutors and from books, I also learnt much from discussions with so many varied fellow students on a variety of subjects both in seminars and casually over coffee.

With a view to widening my experience in preparation for the social work I was hoping to do, I did a variety of jobs in the vacations - working as a nurse, a factory worker, a waitress in a London club, and as an interviewer for the Gallup Poll and for the Ministry of Information. The interviewing jobs often opened up personal confession quite unrelated to the subject under investigation. Alone with a stranger, people would often pour out their heart on subjects which had no relevance to the survey of hearing aids or children's orange juice. But such encounters revealed a great deal about human nature.

In one vacation four of us cycled across Europe to the Passion Play at Oberammergau - a play that brought home the immense impact of the Crucifixion story. It was interesting to see how a vow made in 1869, when the villagers promised to enact this dramatisation of the crucifixion story every ten years if they were spared the plague, is still impacting on life today and now provides a major source of income. On the way home, with less energy, we hitched lifts on lorries and memorably on a barge going down the Rhine, from Heidelberg to Cologne. In those days hitching was a normal way of life and through it I met so many interesting people both as a student hitcher and later as a driver (people often talk quite openly about their lives to someone whom they think they will never see again).

I had gone up to Oxford in confidence that James (the cellist) was on the back-burner. He was the love of my life and I was sure I would never see him again. However within a few days I discovered that he too was at Oxford . . . and playing in the same orchestra. It seemed important not to let a deeper relationship develop, but as neither he nor anyone else knew how I felt, I was secretly able to enjoy making music with him in our rehearsals and yet avoid him at other times.

All seemed to be going well until the third year when I

suddenly realised that James had also evaporated and that I was much more deeply in love with an Australian post-graduate whom I will call Simon. I already knew him well, but it had never crossed my mind that I would fall in love. This time the ecstasy of being in love was tempered by a slight concern about how it would all end but I didn't spend too many sleepless nights over this - he was still around, we both had other friends and life was good.

However this full life all came to rather an abrupt end when, instead of the brilliant degree which my parents and tutor had expected, I scraped through with a poor one. After all their hard work and sacrifice I had let them down. I sank to the depths.

By this time the Groundnuts Scheme which Dr Welch had inspired me to work for, was in ruins and he himself was dead. In any case I needed further training before I could be accepted for any kind of social work. I could not ask my father for any more money; he had two other children to support. I had no alternative but to make the best of a bad situation. My degree in philosophy, politics and economics had included a practical paper in statistics so with this qualification I got the only job I could, with a firm of hospital management consultants. I became part of a team analysing the efficiency of a hospital, even to the extent of applying time-and-motion study to surgeons in the operating theatre! We produced a voluminous report containing information which any competent accountant could probably have told them in a couple of weeks. What futility!

I took a small houseboat on the river at Oxford for a couple of months in the summer to work out what to do next.

A few nights before he left for Australia, Simon came to the boat and we canoed up the river to a pub. When we got back, we said 'Goodbye'. He went away but the love did not. The world went into monochrome and nothing seemed worth doing. I had let my parents down, there seemed no possibility of any meaningful work and now I had lost Simon. For what seemed a long time I was suicidal. It was only the realisation that my parents loved me and of how much it would hurt them which restrained me. It could be said that it was their love which saved my life, although they knew nothing about the way I was feeling as I was far from home. I decided I had to get away from it all - to another country. I arranged to go to Finland for a year.

A few weeks before I left for Finland I took my mother on holiday. I was encouraged by my friend Barbara, who for weeks had been telling me what a wonderful holiday she'd had with her mother and how everyone should experience such a special event. So with the small amount of money I had saved from my hospital job, I invited my mother on a holiday to Scotland and the Island of Iona. It rained quite a lot of the time and I ran out of money at the end. Failure again! However, my mother realised, inevitably, what a mess I was making of my life and both then and later encouraged me to think towards a family instead of a vocation, or rather suggested that they were not mutually exclusive. In so doing, she removed one of my stumbling blocks and opened the door to the possibility of a more mature love.

Finland

In total misery and with my mind filled with questions about life, I became a British Council Teacher-Secretary in Finland. The Finnish language is difficult for foreigners to learn so most Finnish professionals need to learn other languages if they are to communicate with other nationalities. When I was there many of the towns and villages organised social clubs to provide English lessons and the British Council provided them with Teacher-Secretaries who taught English and organised some of the social events. My pupils were mainly engineers, doctors, teachers and housewives. Most of them spoke four languages or more and were vastly superior in language skills to myself. I grew to love and admire the Finnish people with whom I lived and it was indeed a healing experience. They were very hospitable although they would often tell you that it took a long time to really get to know a Finn.

It was interesting to learn that the sauna had originally had a sacred significance for the Finns and that in the old days it would be built before the house itself. However, although the sauna was very much part of everyday life (the hot steam of the interior being often followed by a plunge in an icy lake or a roll in the snow), there was no overt religious observation at that time among those with whom I worked. The churches there seemed mostly inhabited by elderly women dressed in black whose focus was on commemoration of the dead who had fallen in the dreadful war in which Finland was pincered between two enemies.

My contract was for a year and I came back to England hoping to find some meaningful work but was immediately plunged into a huge dilemma. I had known Alec as a good friend for some time. He had continued writing to me while I was away and helped to pull me out of my black hole. Now he was asking me to marry him. I was now open to such ideas in theory and indeed he was just the sort of person who would make an ideal husband and whom I would want for the father of any children we might have - kind and loving, scrupulously honest and dependable. He was extremely lovable and I especially loved his laugh. (Maybe this might prevent me taking myself too seriously!) We enjoyed each other's company and shared an interest in promoting international relationships (we had both independently started a peace group at Oxford). But I was not in love with him and however hard I tried, I could not conjure up this magical state of being. Everyone I knew seemed to have a marriage based initially on falling in love and although I knew that this did not always last and that a happy marriage needed to be worked at, I felt at first that it was not fair to Alec to agree to marriage on any other basis. I had fallen in love in the past without warning when I had no intention of marriage; now that I was open to such a step and positively wanted it to happen, it proved completely elusive. For a while I remained undecided, taking what work I could. One of Alec's great gifts is perseverance and I can only be thankful that he persevered. I realised that I could make a commitment to him and that our love would grow in partnership over the years. This is what has happened. In asking me to marry him he offered me a future which has proved to be more fulfilling and happy than anything I could have imagined. Of course we have had our fair share of ups and downs but it has been a good marriage in which love has kept on growing and I now love him more than I can say. I was able to take an interest and a supportive role in his work in the diplomatic service and likewise he has been tremendously supportive in my explorations in later life (more of which in Part Two).

Italy

I felt I needed a bit of time to adjust and earn some money to contribute to our future marriage. I met a girl who had just returned from a teaching post at a convent in Italy and wanted to find a replacement. I was attracted by the aims of the nuns and it seemed that money might be earned in spare time from the Olympic committee just down the road (this proved not to be the case). I took a job teaching English in a convent high in the Dolomites and although there was a serious lack of money (the parents rarely seemed to pay their fees!) it was a valuable experience. The convent was very small, run by three nuns. The nuns believed that their girls should learn mainly foreign languages, as well as something about the culture from which these languages came in order to promote greater international understanding. To this end they employed an American and myself teaching English, a German, and a French woman as well as Italians. I think that the staff learnt more from each other than the girls ever learnt from us. For a while we were joined by a Chinese nun who told ne about the happy life of her family in China before the days of Chairman Mao. For part of the time the community also included two white Russians and an Indian priest.

Alec came out to visit me, staying with the ski instructor but enjoying his baths in the convent! We had a few days' holiday together in Venice and, just as years later when we visited Florence and Assisi, we were able to marvel at some of the beautiful art and architecture inspired by the Christian religion.

Marriage

After marriage, Alec and I moved into a flat in London and I used my statistics qualification to get a job with cancer research. But very soon a baby (our eldest daughter, Jennifer) came along and we moved into commuter-belt country.

Although at school I had often felt that it would not be right to bring more life into a world which seemed so full of doom and gloom, I now felt much more positive and optimistic. Perhaps children could *change* the world - and be a cause for hope! I began reading books about Natural Childbirth and going to relaxation classes as well as trying to read 'the right sort of books' and see the 'right sort of films' in the belief that these would influence the child in the womb. As each child arrived (I had four) I felt intense love and joy - almost akin to falling in love.

Bringing up a family is a steep learning curve and we have learnt so much from all of our children. In retrospect it is easy to think how we might have done things better, but we simply did as we thought best at the time. I do not talk about the children in this book although I have probably learnt more from raising them than from anything else. Their lives are an integral part of my journey but it would need a book fifty times this size to begin including that. And they have their own stories.

On our Travels

Alec was particularly interested in working in those countries which had gained their independence from the old British Empire. Our aim to foster international understanding in these countries was easier than I had anticipated because almost always there was respect and affection for the memory of British people. However, there was much to learn about other religions, ways of life and differing perceptions of the world which were not always immediately obvious.

In 1960, Alec was offered a posting to Singapore and we travelled out by sea with a daughter of four and a son (Anthony) of two.

After four years (and the arrival of two more children - Rosalind and Michael) in this vibrant multi-cultural island we moved on to Pakistan which provided, amongst many other things, the opportunity to learn about Islam. After three years there, we then had a home posting which enabled us to introduce the children to a normal English education. While in England I was able to teach English to Pakistani women in Woking who led lives of almost total isolation from the surrounding community. Our local church celebrated 'One World Day' in a big way and this drew out fifty-two different nationa-lities living in our town, many of whom had never been noticed before!

Rhodesia

We then had about six months in what was then called Rhodesia (now Zimbabwe). Proposals had been worked out by the British government and Ian Smith, the Rhodesian Prime Minister, to introduce a revised constitution giving Africans some measure of self-government and Lord Pearce led a commission (in which Alec was involved) to see whether the people would accept it . . . which they didn't.

While there, we had the opportunity to visit different parts of the country and meet some of the rural communities. I was impressed by the buoyant sense of humour, the laughter and resilience of so many of the country women who, with no education were struggling to feed, clothe and bring up their children in hopes that they would go to school. I could understand the African saying that 'it takes a village to bring up a child'.

Very often we would see the women working in the fields, some with babies on their backs, while the men sat under a tree playing cards. The women too had their own community activities: we attended various country gatherings where there had been a competition to produce the best cake or the most creative craft work. Each entry was carefully considered and even when some piece of craft work was a total disaster the adjudicator would say, "Mrs Obolonga - You have tried." (Thereafter I would look at one of my own failed bits of knitting and hear her voice saying, "Mrs Ward - you have tried.")

Sri Lanka

Soon after we left Rhodesia we were posted to Sri Lanka. Here the Buddhist, Hindu, Muslim and Christian religions were all in evidence.

I was particularly impressed by the deep serenity in the faces of huge statues of Buddha, some carved in stone and others in painted wood; some standing erect and strong, others reclining with a serene smile. What was also impressive was the way that this serenity seemed to be passed from statue to worshipper as he or she gazed intently at the face in a state of meditation. This transference of a state of mind is something which I later learnt in India is called 'Shaktipat ' - and can be conveyed by guru to sannyasin (or pupil) simply by being in the presence of, and honouring, that person, rather than by any teaching or even touch.

I wanted to learn more about meditation and remember gazing for a long time at a small, seated, stone, Buddha at the sacred site of Polonnaruwa, feeling an inner peace touching me at a deep level. The full moon puja (meditation) was a special time.

A Tamil friend took me to a Hindu temple in Jaffna which left me full of wonder but also incomprehension as I struggled to understand the significance of the various ceremonies which were taking place. However, it was through the Hindu religion that I realised the sacredness of sexuality, something which the Christian religion has missed. After all, sexual union is the source of all human life. The ancient patriarchal Christians, with their vows of celibacy, regarded sexuality as a sin, and by association women as the cause of sin, and our Western civilisation has been plagued by guilt and fear as a result.

Mauritius

From Sri Lanka we moved to what I think is the most beautiful and spiritually potent island in the world - Mauritius. Here on a small island in the middle of the Indian Ocean are gathered many of the different nations and cultures of the world. Obviously there are tensions but, while we were there, the leaders of the various communities were co-operating to learn about each other's religions and to join in celebrating each other's festivals. If only all the world could be like this.

Sometimes I went to St Colomba's presbyterian church with its American pastor and sometimes I went to St Paul's Anglican church or the cathedral. For a long time I had found that one of the obstacles to prayer was that my mind was leaping round from one thing to another. Someone pointed out that yoga could help with this; by stretching and balancing the body into a state of relaxation this would reflect on the mind to bring clarity and integrity between body, mind and spirit.

So I started to learn yoga. In the first lesson our teacher told us that if we practised faithfully every day we would find that by the end of the year it had changed our lives. I took this seriously and found that by the end of six months, life had already changed and that it was possible to hold the mind steady and focussed, to relax deeply and to become aware of a new wholeness.

A seminal experience began in 1978 when I became part of a group of women who met for lunch on alternate Tuesdays. It was initiated by Mary who was an American psychologist. The group included two Muslim women, a Hindu, two Roman Catholics (one of whom was my yoga teacher), a New Zealand Anglican and a Chinese Buddhist psychologist, as well as myself. Others joined in from time to time. We did not discuss religious differences but operated on the heart level. We took it in turns to introduce books about birth, marriage, death, education, health, evolution etc., and then discussed these issues. What came through very strongly was that we had all had the same kind of experience as women and yet we were viewing these experiences of life through the lens of our own culture. We did not always agree, but we all learnt from each other and we sat in a circle, although without the intentional ritual of circle which I came to know later. We were all about fifty years old so had half a life-time's experience behind us. Some of us were also involved in working together for the residents of a home for the disabled (mainly polio victims), providing for undernourished children in country villages and promoting women's literacy. We worked together because we cared about these people and the issues involved. This outweighed any religious differences and we all cared most of all about the kind of world in which the next generation would grow up.

One of the books we discussed was Teilhard de Chardin's *The Future of Man*. Teilhard was a palaeontologist and Jesuit priest who for many years worked in China doing scientific research. As a result of his combined disciplines of science and religion he realised that evolution was an ongoing process. We were not at the top of the tree. He foresaw that humanity was moving into a new evolutionary stage which could be as big a change as the leap into language. I found this an enormously exciting idea. It seemed to explain so much.

It all culminated in an event which drew all these ingredients together and blew me into a much bigger world. A friend, who was being welcomed into a local Anglican church as their new priest, invited me to attend his induction service. This would involve taking the eucharist[15] and saying the creed[16]. I have always been mercifully foggy about my beliefs but knew that I could not subscribe to anything so archaic and alien to my thinking as the creed which I would be expected to say. I went to the bishop and said that I would like to support my friend and take part in the service, but that there was no way I could say the creed. Fortunately he asked me what the eucharist did mean to me, and, rather off the top of my head, I said that for me it would be a commitment to Christ, a linking in love with all those taking part around the world and with those who had taken part in the past and in the future. He said, "OK. Don't say anything at all. Just do it." And that is what happened. It led to an amazing experience.

I was filled with an immense energising love so powerful that without my yoga practice I felt I would have been blown apart. Colours, sounds, scents all became much more intense; I simply became part of a much greater whole and there was amazing synchronicity. I felt immense gratitude and a deep sense of knowing although I could not have put this into words. It was not a 'Damascus road' experience but rather like seeds germinating and growing. From the time when the experience began, memories of my past life would rise from time to time like bubbles from the bottom of a murky pond bursting into full consciousness and I would see them in an entirely different light, until after a few weeks I was seeing the whole world in a new paradigm. It changed my life. This state of heightened perception and energising love lasted for several months and at some level it is there still.

I found that what sustained it was a daily discipline of yoga and meditation, total honesty and following my intuition. However, this amazing experience gradually became overlaid. I suppose I was fortunate to be living in a very friendly environment where those around me accepted what was happening, if not with understanding then with amusement, but I felt that if there had been others in the same state, the resultant creativity could have been enormous.

When this first happened I wanted to try and understand it. I felt sure that there must be some psychological explanation or diagnosis so I searched through the rather limited number of psychology books in our British Council library - but could find nothing. I then searched through other sections and, eventually, in the religious section, I came across books on mysticism and felt a resonance. Although I had not mentioned my search to anyone, a woman who came to our yoga class (whom I barely knew) arrived for a class one day and said, "I think you should read this." It was Maslow's *Towards a New Psychology of Being*. Here at last was affirmation in his description of what he called 'Self Realisation'. The description fitted my own experience although I would have simply described it as 'Realisation' because an essential part of it was complete *loss* of self - a feeling of being simply part of a much bigger wholeness. Yet it assured me that other people were having this kind of experience and consequently that it must have some wider meaning.

While we were in Mauritius, the bishop organised a series of talks considering the questions 'What is the purpose of life?' and the following year 'What is man?' Speakers came from many walks of life and, in a multi-cultural society, from other religions than Christianity. This led me to consider more deeply 'What is woman?'

During this period I also caught my first glimpse of a truth about love which I did not immediately recognise, but which now seems of vital significance. Writing about it thirty years on, it is easier with hindsight to understand. It may have been related to the experience I have just described. I fell deeply in

love. It was with a friend whom I will call Paul, who had introduced me to the books of Teilhard de Chardin (although he
himself was not convinced) and was exploring ways of
finding a new understanding of Christianity relevant to our
modern life. This spoke to my own small quest for finding the
sacred in the wider world. I feel sure it was this common
interest which triggered my love. (I explore other possible
explanations in the chapter on 'Love'.)

It was the last thing I had expected and had I seen it coming
would have made every effort to avoid it. Yet it felt intrinsically
good, true and beautiful, and in some way related to my
Realisation experience.

We are taught that 'falling in love' threatens any existing relationship although I knew that, as I was very happily married to
Alec, this would not happen.

I talked about it to Alec and we tried to understand. I felt no
physical attraction for Paul, nor any need for a special relationship, and Paul was a loner who certainly did not want this.
Nevertheless it was a time of confusion, difficulty and pain as
it clearly hurt Alec and it was vital that I reassured him that my
love for him was as strong as ever. His attempt to understand
what was happening increased my love for him immensely.
It was very deep water into which I had fallen and before long
I was white-water rafting amidst different perspectives and
situations. However, I had trust in the still point within
and gradually I entered calmer waters and realised eventually
that this love had no place in my life as it was.

After a while I managed to transform the energy. I had sustained the 'Realisation experience' through a discipline of yoga
and meditation. I extended my practice now to include my
love. My love became simply an inner source of gratitude, and
joy, with no place in my outer life, although later it became a
source of energy and inspiration. Many people may find this
hard to believe. Few people have experienced the effects of a
continuing spiritual practice such as yoga so it may not be
understood, but I can only reiterate that this is what happened,

and I suspect there are other spiritual practices which could have the same effect.

After a short while, life continued normally and since both Alec and myself were constantly talking to many different people as part of Alec's work, I talked to Paul when opportunity arose; and when we left the island I wrote to him twice a year until he died, telling him of my own spiritual journey.

I realised at the time that this was no ordinary 'falling in love' and having thought about it more over the years I now identify it as 'inspirational love'. I will refer to it again in the chapter on 'Love'.

Homeward Bound

On our way home from Mauritius we spent some time in India. A few days in Bombay enabled me to visit the Elephanta caves. I boarded a motor boat beneath the mighty Gateway to India and with throngs of other pilgrims went across the waters of the harbour to the island where, hundreds of years ago, priests had carved out a temple in the rock in honour of the God Shiva. Once on the island I ascended the flights of steps bordered by booths filled with tourist paraphernalia on either side, out on to the plateau at the top and entered the cave. The three aspects of the divine: Brahma, Shiva and Vishnu were evident on a huge scale but the cave was essentially dedicated to Shiva. The three faces of destroyer, creator and sustainer were carved from the rock as well as Shiva destroying the demons of ignorance and, most significantly, Shiva as the lover of Shakti-Parvati and fused in one with her; a huge Shiva lingam standing alone; Shiva purging passion of its baser elements. I knew that here was a truth which our Western religion had missed. As a result, the liberation of sexuality in recent years had no sense of the sacred.

From Bombay we went up to Poona and I was able to have several yoga lessons from the great yoga teacher B. K. S. Iyengar. This was a challenging, stretching and often painful experience. I was disappointed that he did not talk about the philosophy of yoga about which he has written so eloquently in his book *Light on Yoga* but of course the essence of yoga is that it goes beyond words. The main thing I learnt from him that week was that 'meditation is in the posture'. Yoga is not simply a preparation for later meditation but is in itself a means of finding perfect balance and steadiness in a posture which can then extend a deep peace into the reality of everyday living.

While in Poona I also visited the Rajneesh ashram a couple of times. What a completely different experience! Here, coming in off the dusty road (where beggars sat by the wayside, children tugged at my clothes with bright smiles asking for money and salesmen of all kinds peddled their wares), I went in through magnificent wooden doors with brass studs into what seemed to be a chunk of America. Here was friendly, highly organised efficiency as people came streaming in to be registered for the day. They were mostly sannyasins dressed in the flame and orange robes which proclaimed them to be disciples of Bhagwan. Mostly they were Westerners and young, good humoured, friendly, in fact 'glowing' might be a good description. I was able to listen to two of Bhagwan's addresses in the large arena. The first one was taped, but for the second one Rajneesh came in person, after circling round the arena in a large white car. Such a preliminary immediately made me suspicious, especially after the very elaborate security precautions taken by his followers. However, when he entered - a slight figure with a small black beard dressed in white robes and turban, he emanated a presence, a radiance which filled the arena as he greeted everyone with a smiling, silent 'namaste' and took his seat. In a light voice with plenty of humour which evoked gales of laughter, he talked of love: love energised by sex, powered by compassion, full-bodied with the barriers of guilt, fear, anger and moral boundaries removed. It poured in full flood. It rang true. Such love was clearly the essence of happiness. This was what life was really all about. It made the talk of love in our Western churches seem like the waters of life iced over. Here it poured out in full spate and flowed into the hearts and minds of his listeners.

Afterwards, in the canteen serving doughnuts and coffee, or later in the Blue Diamond Hotel about a mile away, where the sannyasins like brightly coloured birds in their flaming robes moved among the pale shadows of grey suited businessmen and sat at tables eating and talking, there was a glowing loving interaction between them which was almost palpable. They had surely found a deep happiness. Yet I was left wondering how it would last. Would the flood recede after some time and leave rocks of jealousy, possessiveness, hurt in a ruined terrain? Perhaps not. For those who were emotionally mature it was surely the elixir of life. But it seemed that most of us are not big enough yet to handle this sort of love.

The ashram also contained workshops based on popular psychology, which appeared to offer a path to emotional growth, large enough to encompass the kind of love on offer. (But how could a psychology based on self throw light on the dynamics of forces acting between people?) I wondered how much of all this was organised by Bhagwan's American devotees and how much he knew or understood what was going on. There were also opportunities here to learn more traditional spiritual disciplines such as Tai Chi and yoga.

One morning, setting off while it was still dark, I went to a session of dynamic meditation. This took place in the big arena, now cleared and open on all sides. Only a few lamps were glowing while about thirty people limbered up and then, as the drum started beating, moved into strenuous deep-breathing movements followed by energetic self-expression. When I was feeling nearly exhausted we were suddenly bidden to stay immobile and this stance was retained in silence for fifteen minutes as I became aware that the dawn was breaking and light was filling the arena. This was followed by a wonderful period of abandoned free dancing which gave a sense of liberation and joy. It was a deeply spiritual experience making me feel fully alive.

In Poona, Alec and I were also able to visit the house where Gandhi lived and learn more about this amazing, humble little man who moved the world by his dedication and non-violence.

We then went over to Madras and visited many of the temples there before going on down the coast to Mahabalipuram where there was a beautiful ancient temple on the shore dedicated to Lord Shiva. For me this was a taking-off point for a visit to Auroville, the visionary city of the future which was inspired by Sri Aurobindo and 'The Mother'.

Sri Aurobindo was an Indian who had been educated in England at the end of the nineteenth century. He worked for Indian independence and then, realising that a spiritual life was more important, set up an ashram with his disciples in Pondicherry. He believed that evolution is leading to a consciousness which is both spiritual and supramental - a manifestation of One being. A French woman who saw his face in a dream came to join him and became known as 'The Mother'. Together they proved a spiritually creative power. Their vision was of a city with spiritual dimensions centring round a circular arena and a meditation centre. The Mother stated that 'Auroville belongs to no one in particular but humanity as a whole. To live in Auroville one must be a servitor of the Divine Consciousness.' She foresaw it as 'a place of unending education, constant programme and a youth that never ages - a site of material and spiritual research for a living embodiment of an actual human unity.' She envisaged a population of about 50,000.

This project had hardly started, when Sri Aurobindo died, and it progressed under the spiritual direction of The Mother. Brilliant architects gave their designs, building began and all worked together harmoniously as long as The Mother remained alive. However, after her death, quarrels and rivalry broke out until the whole scheme was abandoned. I walked round the dusty scrubland with only a few goats grazing among the buildings - half finished, but so full of promise. Only a handful of people now remain, living in a cluster of houses with a shop, trying to sustain the vision which inspired it all. Human beings are not yet big enough to accomplish such a task but doesn't it give us clues for what we might become?

We visited other parts of India and ended up in Ooty, high in the hills. I was filled with a need to share some of the ideas which had been forming over the last few years and to see whether my new paradigm of the world had any meaning or relevance to anyone else. The embryo of a book was taking shape and I began to write it in Ooty. I wanted it to be readily accessible to people who lived normal, everyday lives like myself, rather than intellectual thinkers, psychologists and theologians, so I wrote it in fiction form but as a basis for discussion. It was based on my own experience and illustrated my new perception of love.

I wondered if this would resonate with the experience of others.

To bring this chapter to a close I would like to quote from the introduction to this book which I called *The Estuary*.

My twenty varied years with my husband in the diplomatic service gave me the opportunity to meet people from a wide range of life and experience and to discuss subjects from the personal to the international.

Increasingly I was impressed that we were always talking within a framework of thought which was both limiting and self-defeating. The constantly recurring phrase, 'You can't change human nature' led me to wonder 'Why not?'

We are very conscious today of the way evolution has developed up to the present time. But what next?

Fifty years ago it was said with the same assurance 'Man will never go to the moon', as if this was one of the fundamental axioms of life.

Why shouldn't human nature grow? Surely Christ showed us the way - a man divinely human. Then why has human nature changed so little in the last two thousand years? Did we really understand the meaning of His life?

In order to explore new areas of thinking, it is necessary to kick away some of the fundamental assumptions which underpin our lives. This can only be done by the emotionally secure. It is like exploring the other side of the moon: although both sides exist, we cannot see them both at once; to see things from the other side, we must lose sight of earth. It is obviously not an exact analogy, but helps us to recognise that the exploration of ideas which may seem to be in opposition to those already held, does not necessarily try to invalidate our present faith.

So why shouldn't human nature grow?

Is it because we have not considered the possibility and tried to envisage what it could mean in real terms?

Is it because we have studied human beings in isolation but have ignored the forces between them which magnetise and energise?

Is it because woman has adopted man's values instead of expressing her own?

Is it because we are living in a framework of assumptions and thought patterns which are limiting, self-defeating and at least one step away from reality?

Is it because we have become alienated from our roots and primal instincts?

Is it because we have no hope today?

There seems evidence that hope lies in the possibility of immense emotional and spiritual growth. This would be into a world which is beyond our present comprehension and so would be impossible to describe today. But perhaps we can identify the growth points and visualise the early stages of such development.

Although very much aware of my own limitations, I have put some of the ideas which I think need to be explored in fiction form. It is intended as a basis for disagreement, discussion and exploration which I hope it will evoke. It is not for those who are emotionally insecure or who do not wish to question their beliefs. It is intended primarily for small groups of people who know each other well and care about each other - particularly groups of women and families with sons and daughters in sixth form or at university. I very much hope that in these circumstances, an honest and caring discussion may itself be a growth experience.

The book is reaching out to something which only poetry can begin to touch and I often fear to brush the bloom off the butterfly. The issues may be oversimplified, but perhaps this is necessary as a starting point to get any kind of grip on them.

In the belief that truth will come through questioning rather than through propounding answers, the book aims to question and evoke a response - to plumb the depth of thought and emotion below the level of present assumption.

Basically the book is concerned with the meaning of love and what it means to be a woman and the relevance of both for the world today. It is one woman's approach to love, life and religion which I hope may be shared by others.

5

My Story - Part Two

*No wiser now than when I was three
although I've the experiences
and the years to say 'I know'.*

*A three year old is naive but true,
trusting others and their wisdom
with a natural wonder and humility
seeing through pretence and pomposity
knowing all about love: I and Thou.*

Andrea Freeman

*We were made to enjoy music, to enjoy beautiful sunsets, to enjoy
looking at the billows of the sea and to be thrilled with a rose
that is bedecked with dew. Human beings are actually created
for the transcendent, for the sublime, for the beautiful, for the
truthful, and all of us are given the task of trying to make this
world a little more hospitable to these beautiful things.*

Desmond Tutu from the *NPS interviews*, 1994, Ed. Robert Siefel

*Be not afraid
To thrust aside half-truths and grasp the whole*

from *In tune with the Infinite*, Ralph Waldo Emerson

When we arrived home in 1981 my husband had just taken
early retirement, the children had left home and Alec and I
were looking for new beginnings. I was hoping to pursue the
quest for spiritual reality and the meaning of love. Alec had
interests of his own (including woodwork) so he was quite content for me to continue exploring - in fact, as I've mentioned
already, he has been hugely supportive throughout.

(Let me reiterate what I said earlier about the family. Although I have not said much about them, I have learnt much from all four children and continue to learn from them as well as from our four grandchildren, but they have their own stories to tell.)

My first task when we arrived home was to finish writing *The Estuary*. The words came inevitably and inexorably throughout that summer. When it was complete, I was unsure whether to try to get it published as I was afraid it could be misinterpreted and could hurt people whom I cared about. So I made a few copies which I lent to friends in the hope that they would give some feedback. The first responses were very positive so I made thirty more, sewing the batches of paper by hand and binding them in covers made of cornflake packets and wallpaper.

I began lending them to people who I thought might understand - mainly to people I met on retreats. Some disappeared without trace, many came back with really helpful feedback, one was returned with angry condemnation. Over two hundred people read them in the end. Only once was I able to discuss it in a group and this was several years later over a period of about five weeks. I had written *The Estuary* looking forward to a time ten years ahead in 1991 when the events I described could have taken place. Once past this time it felt as though it had passed its 'sell by date' and only occasionally has anyone read it during the last fifteen years.

Returning to the UK aged fifty-one with more than half my life over, I was very much aware that I was embarking on uncharted waters. This was the first time in history that the majority of women could live healthily after the menopause for such a long time, with the opportunity to train and study and perhaps put something back into life. I realised that if I wanted to find the truth about life and love I would need to ask women with at least fifty years' life experience behind them - women who were not afraid to question and who would dare to follow where the questioning led. At the same time I knew intuitively that there was vast untapped spiritual potential among older women which was waiting to be released.

Widening Skills and Experience

But first I decided that I must acquire some relevant skills and widen my own awareness of life.

After my experience of yoga in Mauritius, and briefly in Poona, and knowing what a difference it had made to my life, I began an Iyengar yoga teacher-training class in a cold London gym. Four years later, in 1986, I began to teach in Woking.

I also felt I needed some tactile skill to make physical contact as a channel of healing. I wondered whether to take a full course in massage but after spending time with my friend Jen, who is a professional masseuse, I decided that this was not what I was looking for. A full body massage is not for everyone and I felt that a foot massage could be given not only as a healing technique but as a way of making reassuring physical contact in a much more informal way. So I did a very rapid course in reflexology.

This enabled me to become part of a cancer support group and I was able to participate in a circle of sharing. The circle consisted of about six or seven men and women with cancer, a dietician, a counsellor, a woman who taught relaxation and guided visualisation and myself. There was no charge and no payment. We met in a church hall. Such groups had sprung up all over the country with circles of complementary therapies following the initiative of the Association for New Approaches to Cancer in Bristol. It was sharing on a deep level and often I would hear someone say that they were grateful for the cancer which had turned their life around and made them realise what really mattered. Love was generated in such vulnerability.

In order to understand some of the problems of old age, I helped for a year or two in the local Day Centre and, with my husband, took round Meals on Wheels. On the whole, old age did not seem a happy time but I was impressed by the courage and humour shown by so many - and by the loneliness and sense of futility from which the Day Centre provided brief respite.

I also wanted to train as a counsellor and went to a preliminary weekend and interview. However, although this was interesting and I knew that I could learn much, I realised that I could not work within a framework which seemed to base everything, at one level or another on self gratification. My own life was driven by my search for the truth and the love of family and friends. Many women I know are powered by their determination to help create a more peaceful world, others are seeking to find ways of healing, others simply respond to a need. I know this can be twisted into a framework which says that we are simply satisfying our own needs but that seemed like a travesty of reality. Furthermore, counselling then did not seem to recognise any spiritual dimension. Things have moved on since that time and perhaps I should have looked further, but I decided instead to train as a Samaritan. This gave me a much wider understanding - or at least knowledge - of many different human tragedies. I am still haunted occasionally by some of the mistakes I made, either through misunderstanding the situation or being overconfident in thinking I could cope with a person who needed special expertise. However, it was great to be part of a team of people who by simply caring and listening sometimes saved lives and certainly brought compassion, and frequently light, into lives of depression and loneliness.

One lesser known aspect of Samaritan work is that of 'Befriending'. Anyone who is at continuing risk of suicide may be offered a Befriender who gives ongoing friendship and support. After being a Samaritan for over a year I was asked to befriend someone whom I will call Marilyn. I was chosen because she lived only a few roads away from me and in my inexperience I thought that it would be sufficient simply to call in once a week for an hour or so and be available on the telephone. On my first visit Marilyn told me of a Befriender some years ago who had arrived after breakfast and suggested that they went out together for the day, taking a picnic. Apparently this sort of thing happened several times a week. I immediately realised that I should never have taken this on; my life was far too full of other commitments to be able to give the amount of time which she clearly needed. I knew that just round the corner was a church which had a wonderful support system and was very friendly and caring, but because she was not a Christian she felt excluded. I persevered for a few weeks but realised that I could not give her enough time. I went to my supervisor at the Samaritans and explained the situation, asking if another Befriender could be found and then told Marilyn that someone else would be coming as my other commitments prevented me from giving her the time she needed. It was less than a year later that I heard with dismay and sorrow that she was gone. It had not been possible to find another Befriender and I had never checked up on this. To that extent I felt responsible for her death. She needed more than pastoral visiting. She needed someone who could give her ongoing love and commitment or perhaps a network of supporting friends.

I was reminded of her some time later when I gave a hitch to a man who said he was going down to London to 'murder his girlfriend' whom he reckoned had been unfaithful. During our conversation, as we sped down the motorway, he said he had no time for professional social workers or church people doing good - he needed someone who would love him for himself. And he clearly had no other love in his life - no mother, sibling or friend. He was like a starving man, blindly striking out to try and get what he wanted in a loveless society.

Working with the Samaritans led to a request to help with setting up a hostel for the young single homeless. As I got to know some of the residents I puzzled over how they could find any hope or sense of purpose after spending the first twenty years of their lives in a cold and uncaring world. How could compassion touch someone who was in such an armoured shell, defended by street cred and who perceived any kindness simply as 'a soft touch'. Dave had a picture of animal vivisection over his bed which made me shudder and he surely identified with this. He found kicks - or maybe just escape - in sniffing glue.

St James' Church, Piccadilly

It was about 1983 when my friend Anne asked me to take her to a healing service at St James', Piccadilly. This was a great discovery. In those days the rector was Donald Reeves who was not only aiming to bring Christianity into immediate relevance to the twentieth century, but encouraged spiritual search of all kinds with the result that the church and its adjoining Wren cafe were always humming with spiritual energy and exploration.

I attended a series of lectures there on 'Mary the Mother of God'. After them, some of us felt that there was a lot more to be said and so we followed them up with a discussion group. These sessions strengthened my conviction that we need a much larger vocabulary to talk about love and that we need to reconsider the assumptions made by early theologians and psychologists about the nature of woman. The Christian religion contains no whole figure of womanhood for emulation - a woman to whom the sexual act which creates her child is as sacred as the birth which brings a new human being into the world. Instead of recognising these events as basic to the human condition, there has been a tradition among theologians to put a taboo on them and then have a ceremony in church to redeem the situation.

Beyond Words

After these discussions had run their course I initiated a series of meetings after lunch on Mondays. We met in the little tower room of St James', up a flight of winding stairs where a large portrait of Christ stands symbolically behind a meshed screen, as if pointing out the fact that we could not see him clearly. These hour-long meetings were called *'Beyond Words'* and were a group exploration into the meaning of symbols, rites of passage and ritual.

Inevitably we started by talking. After introductions we would talk about the kind of feelings and experience associated with the topic for the day and then have a brief silence while we allowed symbols to appear in our minds. In theory what happened next would depend entirely on these experiences and contributions. In fact, since there needed to be some symbols available, I usually brought whatever I thought might be needed, and a rough idea of what we might do, and then adapted as required. For example, for thanksgiving we let a flower or a star represent a person to whom we felt grateful and placed these in the centre. It was a small room and we met in circle. There was usually a nucleus of Jean, Glenys and myself but often visitors to London would join in, or church people who were simply curious. One way and another over forty people took part - mostly women.

The subjects we covered were: 1) Thanksgiving, 2) Injury and forgiveness, 3) Intercession and 4) Dedication.

Then over a further seven weeks we celebrated a woman's life cycle as we considered: 1) Birth, 2) Menarche - a girl's first period, 3) Vocation, 4) Marriage, 5) Pregnancy, 6) Menopause, and 7) Death. For our last session, a mime artist, Peri Aston, came and gave a symbolic performance in the church of a woman's quest for spiritual truth. (Many of these ideas were developed later in circle and I describe them more fully in the next chapter on 'Spirituality'.)

Resource Groups
Later in the afternoon, after a cup of tea, we moved to the Wren Cafe[17] (or sometimes to the garden on fine days) and were often joined by others. Here we explored what women have to offer in the spiritual dimension.

We considered setting up 'Resource Groups' of women with

a variety of skills and experience (akin to the Cancer Support groups). We talked about how such groups could be formed, what skills would be required and what training possibilities were available. 'Why women?' we asked.

Women's experience has been side-lined for thousands of years. We explored the considerations which I mentioned in the Introduction. Men, we felt, should always be welcomed in such groups (and maybe some time in the future such groups could comprise equal numbers of men and women). We realised that some aspects of mediaeval theology had damaged woman and maybe we needed to look at ways of healing ourselves as a preliminary where such damage was in evidence.

Many women, we knew, already had the skills, the experience and caring capacity to respond to the desperate needs of our society but they lacked the opportunity for training and the channels through which they could release their potential. Others were already working on their own without the support and multi-disciplinary back-up which a Resource Group would give. Some of those who wanted to come to our sessions could not because they already had commitments, but they sent information about their own work and about already existing healing groups.

We struck a rich vein of spirituality during these explorations and they have a significant potential for future development, so I will share them at some length.

1. Overview

At the first session we talked about the possibility of such groups forming a nucleus in the community which would be available for healing and for emotional, practical and spiritual support. They could also, in themselves, be sources of growing awareness.

When it came to the difficult aspect of finance, we knew that most healing groups would ideally like to offer their services free but in our present society this would not be realistic. Members needed to earn a living. It was suggested that one or two in the group might be fund-raisers in order to subsidise this and donations would also contribute.

We then considered a Resource Group which would extend into a wider field beyond the need for healing, providing home support at times of birth, death and life crises. Such a group could include dance, music, drama and art, both for therapy and for expressing our gratitude and aspirations.

We decided to explore what this would entail and for each of the succeeding weeks we considered some aspect of such a group with, when possible, a leader who had experience in the field under consideration. After this opening session we went on to consider counselling.

2. Counselling

Our group included several counsellors. We acknowledged that this was a very wide field.

Unfortunately, we did not have time to explore some of the fundamental questions such as 'What are the assumptions about human nature on which counselling courses are based?' We wondered to what extent the concept of 'transformation' or 'transcendence' might begin to replace that of 'coping'; whether there was too much emphasis on encouraging the client to become self-sufficient and independent, fitting into our present society, rather than helping him/her to develop mature relationships.

We talked about the quality of listening and considered what to do about those who needed a free counselling service but felt that they did not fit into the right slot. It was pointed out that many of the clergy gave a free counselling service but some felt deterred from seeking help there because they were not regular church-goers and felt assumptions would be made which they could not accept. We wondered whether many seeking counselling were in fact looking for pastoral guidance and assurance - or simply compassion and love.

We noted that the word 'counselling' was sometimes used by various cults and organisations as a cover for proselytising. We also felt that the word 'counselling' had acquired a sort of mystique. But there is also 'intuitive listening' which happens informally and can be an important factor in other therapies, too, such as massage and reflexology. The reassurance of touch and communication in these situations is also relevant.

Some people thought that counselling was often seen as the key to everything without equal attention being paid to the body. In a multi-disciplinary group 'head-work' could be supplemented with 'body-work'.

3. Teaching body-mind integration

We recognised that in the past there have been too many attempts to impose an external pattern of behaviour instead of recognising that the body is the temple of the spirit. Too often there has been a striving to be what one is not, an attempt to obey the commands of an external God, an imitation of Christ at a behavioural level rather than perceiving that the truth is within us and that tuning in to a deeper awareness can lead to spontaneous living from a centre rooted in the truth of a more fundamental process. Isn't it probable that St Paul's cry of 'The good that I would, I do not, and the evil that I would not, that I do' is a symptom of this lack of co-ordination and integrity? Would that he could have had a course in yoga!

In addition to this we know that many anti-social actions (sins) are due to malfunctioning metabolism, to stress, to disease. In our world today, which has become so alienated from nature, we need to take responsibility for our bodies, both in being wise about what we eat and drink and in learning the strengths, weaknesses, tensions and rigidities (which can be reflected in the mind), while discovering how to relax, balance, find co-ordination and discover the still centre.

I had invited the yoga teacher Danielle Arin (Lessware) to lead this session but unfortunately she was unable to come. However, she sent me her own experience of yoga teaching which is in the Appendix to this book and which I do recommend you to read.

4. *Teaching meditation*

As soon as we touched on meditation someone immediately said that as soon as she sat down to meditate all the unresolved problems of her life came rushing to the surface making it impossible. This is not unusual when relaxation lifts the barriers which have been suppressing all kinds of material from the past. Such experience underlines the need to combine meditation training with counselling and body-mind integration. Someone suggested that meditation should be rooted in a deep ethical underpinning or it could be dangerous.

We tried to define the difference between contemplation and meditation. (This is considered in the next chapter on 'Spirituality'.) The moving meditation of Tai Chi and the 'meditation in the posture' of yoga both overlap here with the body-mind integration which we had considered previously. We did not have time to talk about healing meditation nor about verbal prayer.

A network of meditation groups, which began in 1973, was named 'The Julian Meetings' after Julian of Norwich.

5. *Healing*

Beverley Martin[18] visited our group to tell us how the Healing Ministry at St James' had been founded four years earlier after nine months of meditation and prayer by a group which gradually grew in numbers. She emphasised that it grew naturally, responding to need. It combined scientific expertise with loving care, and with the realisation that healing was a process in which the 'patient' was also involved. It was often through sickness or trauma that new life could come. The concept of 'the wounded healer' was very relevant. She told us that there were now four main channels of Healing at St James':

1. The Green Room where practitioners were available during the week by telephone for services in counselling, healing and natural therapies.
2. Healing Clinics, held on alternate Thursday evenings in the Rectory.

3. A Walk-in Help and Advice Service from the Peace
   Caravan in the courtyard which was open every day.
4. A service of 'laying on of hands' once a month.

In addition to this there were sometimes whole days of 'healing in the market place' and a number of support groups.

Beverley reminded us that the groups were rooted in prayer and although they took into account body, mind and spirit they were primarily concerned with the spiritual aspect revealed in Christ. They also incorporated Sufi understanding and the light given by all the seven great religions of the world. Mutual support within the group was obviously necessary and we discussed to what extent therapy external to the group, on a regular basis, was helpful or necessary. Both men and women were part of the Healing Ministry and their concern was for the whole person.

We recognised that the techniques of some holistic therapies could be learnt fairly quickly but sensitivity and awareness come only through experience and might need to be combined with scientific knowledge and skill.

Marion pointed out that many healing groups seemed to exist in a kind of limbo ignored by both the Church and the medical profession. But increasingly doctors were willing to recommend such groups as a supplement to treatment of a more traditional kind and the Church was beginning to form its own groups although only in a very limited way.

6. *Music and dance in healing and liturgy*

There is a long tradition of music in the Christian church: plain song, Gregorian chant, organ music, choral singing in oratorio, hymns and psalms - but there has been little dance. Our concern at this session was to consider how all aspects of music could be used in healing and liturgy.

Sylvia Mehta led our discussion. She is reviving the Troubadour tradition and sings and writes songs herself as well as teaching circle dance. She told us how a true song written from the heart can open up the hearts of listeners. It springs from personal experience, but is not written just for the song writer but with a far wider relevance. It can be written for a special occasion such as the birth of a child, or for someone who is going through a difficult period showing where hope lies and perhaps in symbolism showing the way through.

Sylvia said that she thought the songs were given to her for healing. They can also be visionary and give hope in darkness. There are some songs which, when sung together can break down barriers and create a sense of unity.

Anne recalled that Elizabeth Kubler Ross's workshops on death and dying usually began with song for this purpose.

Sylvia spoke of various different ways in which sound can be used apart from its musical content, such as when a group of people each hum their own note and may gradually blend this into a common tone (Yehudi Menuhin also speaks of 'the acceptance of dissonance').

The vibrations of a note of music can vary the shape of a candle flame and can produce patterns in sand on a plate, so the effects are far more than the conscious mind can comprehend.

The texture of the sound is as important as the pitch. Rudolph Steiner gave Eurythmy as a form of healing movement to enable the sounds of music and speech to be expressed through bodily gesture. In nearly all ancient traditions the forms of the visible world were held to be created by the Divine Word, the Logos principle. Eurythmy is based on the perception that the sounds of human speech and of music have in their own manner and degree something of the same formative power. Eurythmy brings this creative principle to expression through gesture and movement.

Sylvia told us of Bernard Vosein who collected circle dances from all parts of Europe and started teaching them at Findhorn. Apart from the co-ordination and healing which this promotes, it also releases emotion and raises the energies which can be directed in healing beyond the immediate participants. There is important symbolism is these dances, too, in taking from the past with the left hand and giving to the future with the right.

Song and dance can enrich ceremonies and rites of passage.

7. *Poetry and drama*

Peri Aston was unfortunately unable to lead our discussion but came to give a performance at the last session.

We heard how a group of four women conducting a 'One World service' had used drama to draw the contrast between breakfast time in the west and breakfast time in a developing country. The service also included a poem written as a despairing cry of an African mother whose child was dying of starvation. Poetry can lead us powerfully beyond the meaning of the words themselves.

Although there is poetry in the psalms and hymns, we felt that a critical reappraisal of both was needed and that much more use could be made of modern poetry. Liturgy itself was originally a form of drama. The Passion Play at Oberammergau and the York Mystery Plays were mentioned.

Drama during a church service has usually meant the enactment of a biblical story, often by the Sunday School, but it has a far wider application.

Patte told us about her experience of *psychodrama* and the dramatically healing effects this could have. She underlined the need for this to be done in a group where there was love, acceptance and support and under the direction of a trained leader. It could clear blockages, release emotion and bring new understanding of relationships.

Anne told us of '*fairy tale workshops*' in which everyone wrote their own fairy story and then chose others to act out the parts with them. She described the emotional release and insights which could come from this. We wondered to what extent our fairy tales and dreams used the material in which we had been brought up as a symbolic vocabulary and how much it was something generic to a common consciousness.

We did not have time to discuss the prophetic role of drama:

how it might be used to give a vision of future potential and reveal hope in a world of fear.

8. Art

We spoke of the architecture and sacred geometry of church buildings and noted the significance of the dome as opposed to the tower or steeple. As an American visitor, Patte commented on the amount of military symbolism in our churches and cathedrals. Glenys pointed out that the feminine symbolism was there too but hidden. She told us of the Shropshire church-yard where there is an ancient Celtic cross with the centre of the cross encircled to represent wholeness and above this the Mother Goddess. We looked at pictures and photographs of Silbury Hill and the figurine of the Mother Goddess from the same site. Anne showed us a picture of Visica Pisces - two linked circles from the chalice well in Glastonbury.

We heard about Yvonne's weekends where a theme such as 'Thine is the kingdom' was expressed in various art forms and then the finished models or paintings were used for contemplation. She thought that there would be an increasing number of such workshops.

Painting and Prayer Retreats at various centres round the country provide a type of meditation by giving the opportunity to look at something in depth, both in detail and as a whole. It can be a way of creating inner stillness and this may be more important than any finished result.

We heard how painting could be used in a therapeutic way as a means of expressing feelings which could not be expressed in words and how such paintings should be allowed to speak for themselves without verbal interpretation. Patte had used modelling on weekends for family retreats when each member of the family would be asked to reveal feelings of isolation, rejection or linking which had previously been unrecognised.

Anne thought that pottery is a craft which has its own integrity without reference to liturgy or healing. Children will often talk very freely while they are absorbed in making a pot, which gives it a secondary therapeutic value.

We did not have time to consider the sort of criteria which make a painting or model appropriate for exhibition. There may be a need to disturb or stimulate; there may also be a need to express something which is deeply felt and which has not yet found a means of expression, but this also stimulates a response in the spectator and, particularly in the context of healing, perhaps more consideration could be given to the vulnerabilities of spectator groups? When is a painting more appropriate for a therapist than for an exhibition?

Anne spoke of the new figure of Christ on Wells Cathedral and the experiences of the sculptor in making this.

9. Care of the dying
We began by considering the needs of the bereaved, the need for someone to listen and just be there - to be able to cope with the anger as well as the grief, without rationalisation or projection of personal theories about life and death. Many people are too frightened of death or feel they are not adequate to help someone who is bereaved - those who do come may be turned away by anger, yet this holding back can make the bereaved person feel isolated or even ostracised.

We heard of the desolation of a mother who was informed of her son's death in the small hours of the morning and was then just left by herself. If there were a resource group of women who could be called on when such an emergency arose, one of them might be able to accompany the policeman on this sort of mission.

It was emphasised that it is a matter of long-term involvement and not just a brief listening ear. John pointed out that there is also a need to support those who listen. We recognised the importance for the listener to have the discipline of creating a pool of stillness within herself/himself once or twice a day by meditation, perhaps accompanied by some physical exercise which enables the mind to find stillness and empathy. Very often listening to a harrowing story can arouse inner turmoil and in order to protect against this a detachment is deliberately cultivated. However, we were told the story of the yogi who, when a mother brought to him the body of her dead child, had such a deep inner stillness that he was able to empathise totally, with tears streaming down his face, and yet have the strength to give her support. This, however, is something which can only be achieved after years of yoga practice.

Jen reminded us that support in bereavement is already given. Sometimes, if it falls to one woman only, she may be swamped by this kind of caring, but a group of women could do it between them. The advantage of having a multi-disciplinary group would be the availability of various kinds of therapies, especially those involving touch.

We heard from someone who was recently bereaved that she had no patience with the 'professional carer' ('One should not have to pay for love'). What was needed was a really caring person prepared to listen.

Anne spoke of the value of Elizabeth Kubler Ross's work-shops on 'Death and Dying' which often lasted a whole week. Sometimes workshops for the bereaved were too short and although there might be some healing in these between two people who could share their grief, very often the sorrow was too deep-seated to be helped in this way. It takes time and sometimes people could be left feeling exposed and vulnerable without the necessary comfort.

In talking about occasions of cremation and burial, it was suggested that much more scope should be allowed for relatives to arrange the sort of ceremony as they wished (or according to the wishes of the deceased). From experiences mentioned, more latitude may be available than is generally supposed. People are not aware of the options and do not ask. (This sub-ject is considered more fully in the next chapter.)

We considered the need for hospice training which can be obtainable from St Christopher's Hospice and other hospices. A loving compassion is fundamental for training. We recog-nised that, in such places, the concern extends beyond the person who is dying to the family as a whole. Furthermore, a similar kind of support may be required in other cases of loss such as a broken relationship, amputation, loss of a job, etc. We recalled the bereaved man who had come to us recently, asking for someone just to hold him for a time every day while he cried. He had not been able to find anyone in London who was prepared to do this. Sadly we could not help him either. Were we too convention bound or frightened?

10. Support for mother and family at the time of birth
This session was led by a teacher of Natural Childbirth who was already a member of the group.

In the past the mother of the pregnant woman would often be present at the birth (and other women too) and would give support afterwards. Too often nowadays the experience is subject to hospital routine and the mother left too much on her own at home afterwards.

It can be important for the husband to be present at the birth, but the woman may need some mothering herself afterwards, as well as help with the child. She may find it difficult to adjust to the change when the baby becomes the centre of attention rather than herself. There may also be problems of jealousy from others in the family which she finds difficult to cope with, quite apart from the exhausting physical demands which a new baby makes on the mother. The condition of post-natal depression is more readily recognised now and there are support groups to help mothers going through this problem.

A young mother can become very isolated as well as exhausted and someone coming to the house to provide a bit of companionship and support, as well as physically helping in the house or looking after the older children, can be very important.

Before the birth it could be helpful if someone from the group were able to teach relaxation and provide the opportunity for some free time if there are older children. Of course we knew all this but we needed to review what such a resource group could be asked to provide.

11. Youth support and voluntary service

It would have been useful to have explored more fully than time allowed what a group of women could offer to the young, especially the unemployed. There are so many desperate needs in our society which could be met by the skills and abilities of the young unemployed if it were not for economic constraints. There is also a need to recognise the value of such work in terms of life experience rather than purely in a monetary context. There is still a residue of perception from socialist thinking that any voluntary work is exploitation of the workers.

There could be informal teaching of basic life skills: nursing, cooking, mothercraft, pottery, car maintenance, household accounts, painting, instrument playing etc., by those who, from their own experience and training, could open new doors. Kate suggested that a woman from such a group might visit sixth-forms to talk about sex education in a wider perspective of adult life and relationships.

A listening ear and affirmation of skills, hopes and dreams can be very powerful. There could also be scope for mentoring.

12. What next?

In our last session we thought about future meetings and there was some discussion as to whether these should just be for women with half a life-time's experience behind them or for everyone. We discussed it with Beverley and Ranjan from the Healing Ministry. I suggested exploring the rhythms of the menstrual cycle and the menopause and how we could tune into these. Ranjan said that men had rhythms of life too and both he and Beverley wanted it to be open to all. We considered exploring the rhythms of life on a broader perspective, eg, the rhythms of the day, then the week, the month, the year and a life-time. We thought that perhaps we might be able to identify some of the underlying factors, start learning how to tune in with these rhythms and observe how they linked up with the rhythms of prayer life and meditation.

At the end of this series of meetings, as I mentioned above,

Peri Aston, a mime artist, gave us a brilliant performance of a play which she had written herself called 'Quest'. She performed this in the church with a backdrop of a copper sun overlaid by the crescent moon above the sea.

Beginning with an introduction symbolising the gift of healing and the flying of a joyful rainbow kite, we were introduced to an old tramp woman who reflects on the superficiality of her past and the misery and loneliness of her present.

As she sleeps, Peri takes us back to the dawn of time with God creating the world - a world of life and joy and hope, yet with larger fishes eating smaller fishes - through the Native American Indian legend of the First Woman and the recurring theme of the unicorn, through the three faces of the moon woman and the militaristic sun-worshipping man to the razzmatazz of present day society disintegrating into a cruise missile and the destruction of war. In the end there was the joyful flying of a rainbow kite and healing. It was a feast of symbolism, music and poetry, giving us much to think about and to feel.

In a lively discussion afterwards, Peri told us she had just completed a tour of churches and cathedrals. Peri was one of a group called 'The Holy Fools' who bring clowning and humour into the Church. We spoke of the healing power of laughter and hence the need for comedy and clowning, yet we recognised that laughter can be cruel and that maybe we need to consider more carefully what we are laughing at. Someone pointed out that laughter could reinforce attitudes which were not necessarily healthy.

Apart from this last session, all our sessions had been small - never more than nine and changing - but included women from America, Canada, Australia, Norway, France and Holland, as well as from many other parts of England. We hoped that such ideas would continue to be discussed in these and other areas. Perhaps some of our circles might evolve into Resource Groups.

The Abbey, Glastonbury

However, a couple of hours a week in session at St James was really not enough. So, very much following my intuition, the next step was a weekend retreat at the Abbey House in Glastonbury at Advent. I had been to the Abbey House before this on a Painting and Prayer Retreat. I loved Glastonbury and although my painting skills were minimal, it had been a great opportunity to sit among the ruins of the old abbey and really look and think and absorb the atmosphere and the history.

On this 'Painting and Prayer' visit I was looking through the visitor's book and came across a page headed 'Blue Pilgrims'. While abroad I had read about a woman called Beatrice Hankey who in the 1920s had a mystical experience in the Lake District which changed her life. She then realised that her vocation was not to aim for women's ordination but rather to set up her own women's ministry independently. Consequently she gathered some friends around her and went off to the Welsh mining villages where families were suffering as a result of the 1926 strike. She brought food, comfort, support and the gospel to men, women and children. She and her friends wore blue veils and so were called 'Blue Pilgrims'. What a pity that was so long ago, I thought, and imagined that now it was all defunct. But no! Here they were! I made contact and was invited to visit another Sheila in Devon. It was not what I expected. Yet I found the *Aquarian Conspiracy* lying on her table so guessed we would be on the same wavelength.

The Blue Pilgrims now were not just a women's ministry as I had thought, but in fact part of a group calling themselves 'The Knighthood' which included men and women as well as children. I had been brought up on the legends of King Arthur, and the central quest for the Holy Grail. However tenuous the links with history might be, these legends as least gave us insight into the intuitions and yearnings of our ancestors, and the search for the Holy Grail represented for me the search for wholeness and had immediate relevance to our own time.

The fundamental cause of such a loss of wholeness was the wound in the groin of the Fisher King. As long as this remained unhealed the whole land was barren. For me this represented man's damaged perception of women and the denigration of the act of sexual fulfilment. Although this is an expression of the deepest love between two people as well as the initiation of new life, it has not only been trivialised but positively denigrated, with the word for such activity being used as a swear word and many spiritual leaders being debarred from this altogether by their celibacy.

In the version of the story which I was told at school, one of the most perfect knights, Perceval, had been sent to ask a question which would bring healing, but when he got there he could not think what to say! Then an old woman in the crowd asked the direct question, "What ails thee?", which was the first step in the healing process. As a result of this the barren land became fertile and the Grail became available.

The Blue Pilgrims/Knighthood now were Christians who called themselves 'Learning Knights' as they sought to understand and live the way of Christ. They included among their members, an inspirational scientist called Claude Curling, whose papers I had read while we were abroad. So in a different way I had found what I was looking for. I was invited to the next retreat at Glastonbury and given a warm welcome. Many of them read my book 'The Estuary' and gave helpful feedback. As part of each retreat we have a Round Table during which each of us tells about the progress of our particular 'quest'. So here I was again, sitting in a sacred circle . Over the years they have given great support. So it seemed appropriate that our advent retreat of women from St James should be at Glastonbury.

About twelve of us sat in circle and those who had special skills such as teaching Tai Chi, or leading a visualisation session, or playing the piano and singing, led sessions. There were some creative contributions but, on the whole, it felt a very uncertain start to our exploration - although it had its hilarious moments! I organised another weekend at the same time the following year. Whatever the shortcomings, it convinced me that we needed to pursue such explorations, preferably with three-day weekends and I realised that the ideal way to do this would be to have our own retreat house where I hoped I would be able to invite women to come to share the exploration as guests - or at least with only a small donation.

Mothers for Peace

While at St James' I heard about 'Mothers for Peace'. This was an organisation started by a woman called Lucy Behenna, an unmarried school-teacher then in her eighties. She had been working for peace all her life, but this resolve was intensified after an experience taking refuge with children in an air-raid shelter when a doodle-bug bomb had come over and narrowly missed them. She vowed that she would do all she could to make sure that no children had to go through such an experience again. So during the Cold War, when things were looking black and she was in residential care in Crawley, she had the idea that if all the mothers of the world got together then there could be peace. No one took her seriously to begin with, but finally they did and she set off on a pensioners' ticket to talk about her idea round the country and to raise the money for such a project. Eventually with the money she had raised, which included all her life savings together with grants from the Quakers and other Peace groups, she was able to pay for eight young mothers to go on a peace mission. The Quakers helped to select them and organise the expedition. Four went to the Soviet Union and four went to America and then they came back and talked about their experience. The following year, mothers from the Soviet Union and USA came to England.

I found it an inspiring story and although I was no longer a young mother, I offered to write a biography of Lucy. Despite the fact that I was such a newcomer, they kindly accepted my offer and the research for this little book enabled me to meet many wonderful Quakers and peace campaigners. These were men and women whose lives were dedicated to peace and their constant refrain was, 'Let there be peace on earth and let it begin with me,' as well as, 'Peace will come through the will of ordinary people like yourself'. As I looked into the sometimes austere yet kindly faces showing such gritty courage and determination I could feel that here was the real hope for the future. Many had gone to prison as a result of their peace protests, but it wasn't all just a matter of protest but of welcoming and befriending the 'enemy'. Transforming the 'enemy' into a friend who, as a mother, shared the same concerns and passionate desire to create a peaceful world in which children could live and love and grow, was a vital part of their philosophy. As part of this research I joined a group of women going to the Soviet Union in order to try to meet some of the Soviet women with whom Lucy had made contact. This proved to be difficult as there was still great suspicion of Westerners and fear that contact would be dangerous. It was an opportunity to learn about the Soviet way of life and see some of the ancient and modern buildings but it was not until I later met a group of Russian women at our home in the UK that it felt possible to become friends.

Greenham Common

It was also at this time that I was able to visit Greenham Common. This was the site of an American nuclear-missile base in the south of England which for years, since 1981, had been the centre of women's protest. Women had come on peace marches from all over the country, set up camp in benders and tents around the base, protesting by blocking the entry road with their bodies and singing peace songs. They had been a continuous presence for several years and many had been arrested and spent nights in prison. Most of them were law-abiding housewives and mothers who would never have dreamt that they would see the inside of a prison. It was a significant movement for raising women's consciousness and empowering women in a much wider way than Greenham itself. Whilst at Greenham, I went first to the orange gate and then on to the blue gate, finally settling at the green gate with a bus load of women from Newcastle who had travelled down for a twenty-four hour visit. We sang songs round the campfire and then, joining hands, walked along the perimeter fence. There was a different kind of ambience at each of the gates I visited, but all spoke loud and clear of the power of women in the cause of peace. I pitched my sleeping-bag between the roots of a tree, despite invitations to share a tent, and although I did not sleep much that night I felt humbled and ashamed that I had not played a larger part in the protest.

Peace Pagoda

During these years a Peace Pagoda was opened in Battersea Park, tended by a group of Japanese monks. Around the pagoda hung models of flying cranes which were in memory of the little Japanese girl who, knowing that she was going to die of radiation sickness after the atomic bomb, started making paper cranes as symbols of peace for the world. I can't remember how many birds she made before she died, but it was a powerful message of what one little girl can achieve in the cause of peace. One evening each month there would be a ceremony at the pagoda, organised by the monks who would then lead us all with a beating drum through the streets of London to St James', where we would end up with a cup of tea and a biscuit in the church. Quite why we did this I am not sure, or whether it made any impact on anyone - except ourselves!

India Again

During this time our younger daughter, Rosie, was teaching in Dehra Dun in northern India. I went out to visit her and was able to visit a yoga ashram in Rishikesh as well as seeing the building where the Maharishi taught meditation to the Beatles - now deserted and locked up with an armed guard. It was a sacred experience to walk along beside the waters of the Ganges in the very early morning to a yoga class that took place on the flat roof of the ashram in the dawning light. From Rishikesh, Rosie joined me and we went up the Kedarnath pilgrimage trail which I describe later.

While in India, I was also able to visit a leper colony and to observe the dedication of the staff and the way that some of the leper families not only accepted their condition but aimed to lead a full family life.

The Grange

Meanwhile, back in England, we were looking for a place where women, with half a life-time's experience behind them, could meet and explore together. It seemed that if we sold our house in Woking (which in any case was too big for us now the family had flown), we could buy a much bigger one out in the country (a sad economic truth). My sister, Phyllis, and her husband were running a country house hotel at Ellesmere in Shropshire, so for a couple of years we went to visit them and looked at numerous properties which we considered renovating or adapting. Then in 1986, to my great surprise, Phyllis said that she and Peter wanted to move to somewhere smaller and the house - the Grange - was on the market. It seemed the perfect place, but it was *very* large and all our extended family and friends tried to dissuade us from such a foolish step. Rosie was in India and our sons preoccupied at university or work but our eldest daughter, Jenny, was living nearby and was the only one to encourage us.

In April 1987 we moved in.

The Grange is a beautiful Georgian house in ten acres of gardens, meadow and woodland with fifteen bedrooms. This was an ideal size for what we needed. It was also up and running as an accommodation venue already so that we could start at once. With great trepidation my husband agreed to look after the maintenance of house and garden and without his hard work and support it would never have been possible. Not, in fact, that we had any visitors for some time!

When the Mothers for Peace invited their counterparts in Russia and America to come back to the UK, they normally stayed in private homes and, as yet, they had not been able to stay in one place together. Now that we were going to have this space available, I invited them to come to the Grange for the final weekend of their UK visit. On the very morning we moved into the Grange, I had a letter saying that they would like to come and this seemed to vindicate our decision. They came regularly for a number of years afterwards and later groups included women from Japan, and, on one occasion, women from all parts of Ireland. We met in circle, we shared and laughed and cried and danced and got to know each other. On the first occasion, we planted a tree of peace in the flowerbed opposite the front door and later planted spring bulbs round it in memory of Lucy Behenna, the Mothers for Peace founder - now long dead.

I had hoped that women would flock to take the opportunity to explore the potential of the second half of life, but there was initially little interest and it was not until 1994, after a small paragraph about us had appeared in *Good Housekeeping,* that women began to come in any viable numbers. I should mention, however, that we had some enriching sessions with the ones, twos or threes who did come on earlier weekends. I was doing all the cooking myself at this point so maybe it was just as well!

However, friends who were teachers of yoga, Tai Chi, circle dance, meditation and personal growth came and filled up our programme, attracting many new people on to the mailing list. Charles Shells, the initiator of 'Painting and Prayer Retreats', also came regularly with his painters and with his wife Anne.

Although I was doing the cooking myself for all these groups, I was also able, with much forward planning and preparation, to join in most of them. It was an enriching experience but also involved a steep learning curve. Later on, when the groups became larger, a cook arrived like an angel from Heaven in the shape of Pauline and when she left to continue her studies at university, then Linda arrived to take her place. It seemed to confirm Goethe's assertion that once you are truly dedicated then the universe moves in to help.

For the first few years Kate Money and Ursula Dickenson[19] came in the spring and ran a five-day workshop in which the participants were almost entirely women. It was in these workshops that I really learnt the value of the spiritual circle, with its candle in the centre and an opening and closing ritual. One of the sessions was entitled 'Rites of Passage in a Woman's Life' for women only and, during this, two of us marked our entrance into the second half of life in a ceremony which I describe in the chapter on 'Spirituality'.

I had wanted to invite women as our guests, or only with a small donation, because I felt we were all exploring together. However, because the house was so expensive to maintain (and heat!) this was not possible and we had to begin charging for the weekends simply to cover bed and board (although we always ran at a loss!). However, Elizabeth Staveley, who had come to one of our very early weekends, generously started a bursary fund which, since then, has been added to by other donors, thereby enabling those who could not afford the full fee to come on a much reduced basis.

As the groups became more viable I also felt the need of help. Rosemary Ward, had been to the Grange several times, first with a group on a walking holiday and after that on psychosynthesis weekends. She was already a trained counsellor and was now taking her training in psychosynthesis. As our Second Half of Life group in 1994 was bigger than it had ever been before, I asked her if she would help me with it and she did. We have been working together ever since and, as she embodies many of the characteristics, qualifications and talents which I lack, this is a good arrangement. It is very confusing that she has the same surname when we are no relation - even more so that my daughter who now runs the Grange is called Rosalind Ward-Allen - or Rosie.

Working Weekends

Although Alec worked for eight hours a day (or more!) in the garden and we had help from a gardener, Frank, for one day a week, there was always more to do than they could cope with. So twice a year we held Working Weekends for family and friends. It was good to have the excuse of seeing them all twice a year and in the process we realised what a bonding experience it was to be working together on a variety of tasks and spending the evenings making music. They also worked extremely hard and the house and grounds would not have been the same without their input.

The Eisteddfod

One highlight of our year was the annual musical Eisteddfod in Llangollen. Having been started in 1947 in this small Welsh village, it had brought together musicians, singers and dancers from all over the world to a week of international music-making. All the visitors were found accommodation in outlying villages and Ellesmere took its fair share. Over the years we hosted singers from Ireland, dancers from Turkey, choirs from Greece, Sardinia, Norway and several other countries. We were able to accommodate quite a few of them at the Grange and it was a wonderful opportunity to get to know some of them. On the Thursday evening, after they had finished their competitions, we would usually have a ceilidh at the Grange to which other hostesses from the town came along with contributions of food and at which our visitors would sing or dance for us all and often ask us to join in. It was an illustration of how music can bring nations together and a fulfilment of the Eisteddfod motto which goes:

Byd gwyn fydd byd a gano
Gwaraidd fydd ei gerddi fo

meaning:

Blessed is a world that sings
Gentle are its songs

It is inspiring that a small nation with such talent of its own in song should take the initiative to welcome the world and make such an exciting step towards world peace, and we were grateful to be able to share in the experience.

Exploration at the Grange

During our Second Half of Life weekends at the Grange we have often been able to include an hour or so of song and have had some beautiful solo singers such as Kathy, Angela and Joan, who sang as professionals, as well as musicians such as Val, Kate and Elma, who led us in singing together. Elizabeth brought some musical instruments to lead us in a session and although we always include circle dance in our weekends we have been introduced to other types of dancing which have included belly dancing and the five rhythms of Gabrielle Roth.

We have also been fortunate to learn from those with specialised expertise or experience: Maureen told us of her experience with the 'Alternatives to Violence Project', Maggie and Eileen showed us their own moving meditation, Liz gave us a session on the menopause (on which she runs her own workshops), Susan told us about her errands of mercy to

Bosnia, Barbara and 'Ben' gave us Tai Chi lessons, Jeanette gave us a lesson in yoga, Georgina showed us a way of communicating through drawing, and Jean taught us a way into meditation. These are only a few of the riches which were given so freely over the years and from which I, and others, have gained so much. It was all very much intrinsic to our exploration.

Moving On

As the century drew to a close, our younger daughter, who was at the time living in London with her husband was thinking of moving into the country to start a family. About this time the last of the bantam hens which had belonged to my sister finally died. (Never underestimate what may seem to be a trivial event!) They had never given us any eggs but it had always seemed a pity to end their lives prematurely! The hen house was now available and Rosie and Jon realised that this would convert into a good office for their specialised publishing business. They came to live nearby and took a great interest in running the Grange. At the millennium I was seventy and my husband was seventy-two: it seemed time for us to retire for the second time. So Rosie and Jon, now joined by their two little girls, moved into the Grange to take over from us, which they have done with great hospitality and imagination. At this time our eldest daughter and her family were moving out of their house in Dorset to an overseas posting and so we were invited to house-sit for them. This has been a good arrangement as Rosemary and I are still able to run our Second Half of Life Explorations without all the hard work of running the Grange and Alec has been relieved of the burden of house maintenance - although he still enjoys tending the many trees he planted while in residence and single-handedly re-glazing the Victorian greenhouse. We travel between Shropshire and Dorset fairly frequently.

In Dorset I have joined a United church which is an open-minded community of men and women. Their Vision statement contains no package of beliefs but welcomes everyone, valuing our diversity whatever our age, background, culture, gender or race, recognising that we each have something to share with others. Together we 'seek personal and spiritual growth for ourselves and others, to care for and support each other within and beyond the church community' . . . and 'the wider world by caring for the earth, striving for a just and peaceful world, identifying with the poor and the powerless'. It is a thriving community with plenty of music - a spiritual centre geared to the future.

Our congregation go to church for different reasons. People sometimes assume that I go seeking protection from a higher being, which is not so. Or they think I am looking for salvation and a guarantee of life after death which is also not the case. I go because it is good to belong to a caring community, with a love which extends beyond the church itself to the lost, the marginalised, and the lonely. I realise that the love of God can more effectively manifest in a community rather than just through individuals who may get caught up in the trammels of 'need love'. We need to learn a lot more about the various aspects of love, about communication and about creating an inner stillness but these are all thing which we can explore within the church. Basically, in my perception we are being transformed from a society of individual human beings looking for our own happiness, salvation, or security into a community working for a higher good. Such a process could be taking us to a whole new way of being.

For the first few years of our 'freedom' Rosemary and I tried taking our explorations to other retreat houses in Leicester, Glastonbury, Sutton Courtenay and Woking. However, for the time being at least, we have decided to be focussed on the Grange.

Many of those who had been on our explorations wanted to come back for another weekend, so after a while we began to hold 'Further Exploration' weekends each July. This enabled us to start at a deeper point and explore more on a spiritual level.

Sophia means female wisdom and it seemed appropriate to call those who wanted to keep in touch and pursue this search for wisdom 'Friends of Sophia'. We have a twice yearly newsletter called 'Sophia'. There are now quite a large number of Friends from all parts of the country and some are now starting their own local groups.

It seems that our circles at the Grange and our expanding circles of Friends of Sophia may be part of a much wider movement towards wisdom which I hope the present book may serve to extend.

I hope too, that such circles will also be able to explore the various varieties of love and bring the thoughts which I express in the chapter on 'Love' to maturity. These circles can be like nests which are gradually strengthened by love and trust. They are capable of hatching out eggs of new ideas such as the varying concepts of love and the meaning of 'Realisation' and bringing them to reality. As I said earlier, I see them as the embryonic cells of a butterfly which will usher in a whole new way of being.

6

SPIRITUALITY

Wisdom does not come until 'we are ready to take upon
ourselves the mystery of things'

Helen Luke

The quest for spirituality is the quest for humanity.

Ursula King quoting Skolimowski

The time of the lone wolf is over. Gather yourselves!
Banish the word 'struggle'
from your attitude and your vocabulary.
All that we do now must be done
in a sacred manner and in celebration.
WE are the ones we've been waiting for.

Hopi Nation, Oraibi, Arizona

My initial quest had been to find a spirituality which related to
our life experience. Our explorations have produced a rich
harvest, some of which I would like to share

What is Spirituality?

Our groups at the Grange include women from various faiths
or none at all. It is important that in this area we do not operate on a 'head level' with argument and discussion but rather
from the heart. We can all ask questions. We can all share
silence and symbolism. We can all speak from the truth of our
own experience. Above all we can all aim to increase our capacity to love. Spirituality runs through all religions and in
seeking to deepen our awareness of this we in no way oppose

any existing faith but rather contribute our insight and experience as women to deepening this aspect.

When we speak of 'finding our spiritual path', the first reaction is sometimes: 'Whatever do you mean by that?' or 'I am sure I have no such thing'.

For some people in the past, the 'Spiritual Life' simply meant preparation for life after death: leading a good life now in preparation for the Hereafter. But increasingly we are aware of the spiritual dimension within the present - the awareness of timelessness or a sense of being beyond time when we tap into the profounder depths of life. This is to do with the quality of life here and now - if it extends beyond the grave, so be it.

My own search - also expressed, although in different ways, by many of the women who come to explore - is compounded of a yearning for something beyond myself, a wonder at the immensity and beauty of the world, together with a deep gratitude - a conviction that love and the search for truth are innate, and that such natural yearnings are gateways to a richer and deeper quality of life - a search for wholeness.

Spirituality is finding the sacred in all things, from a drop of dew, to the flight of a seagull, finding the sacred in each other (as a basis for love) and continually discovering more of the sacred within ourselves - recognising that we are all one.

It is moving beyond words into silence, beyond chronological time into the eternal present and becoming aware of the value of NOW.

It is sharing the rich symbolism of existing ceremonies as well as creating rites of passage, ceremonies and blessings from music, poetry, symbols and dance. Such ceremonies can be created together to form outward signs of inward events and so affirm and anchor them in life and community.

I suppose that essentially this comes down to our search for a meaning in life, trying to make sense of what it is all about and finding a deeper purpose. This is what is felt by many of the women who come to the Grange. Today there is a thirst for meaning among all sections of the population and especially among the young which, when unsatisfied, leads too often to depression and suicide. For many, the search is continuous, for there are always deeper meanings and new insights, but for some there comes a time when we discover an interpretation of life which rings true (usually among huge clouds of unknowing!) and our path depends on how we follow this light.

For some, a ready-made belief system may provide an adequate framework in which to live out life, but for others there is questioning and testing against experience and accepted knowledge until there comes a point where it is possible to find an integrity within, and an awareness of something beyond our present understanding - maybe simply a sense of the direction in which we could be moving. It is important that when/ if we believe we have found a belief structure which is true for us, we still keep an open mind and do not try to impose our beliefs on others.

I consider in this chapter some of the concepts which we have encountered in talking about the spiritual dimensions of life and how these relate to some of the rites and ceremonies which can be created in circle.

Ethical Foundations

The foundation of any spiritual life is integrity.

The three great Western religions of Judaism, Christianity and Islam have all based their morality on the ten commandments which Moses believed had been given to him by God. These have proved a useful guide to outward behaviour over the centuries. But this is not the *only* code, although most of the precepts would be accepted as a basis by most religions. There is also Confucius' rule of thumb: 'Do unto others as you would that they should do unto you' (or, more precisely, it seems he said, 'Do not do unto others as you would not have done to you') - 'Do as you would be done by'.

Then there are the five Yama and the five Niyama of the yoga philosophy of Patanjali (see Appendix under 'Yoga'). These precepts relate much more to the ground from which our actions spring and give direction on how to cultivate such attitudes in a physical way. The first precept is 'ahimsa' - 'non-violence', which covers so much more than 'Thou shalt not kill'.

In a feminist reaction to the sense of duty imposed by a male culture, it is fashionable today to discard all the 'shoulds' and 'oughts', especially the inherited ones - but I would be loathe to banish these words entirely from our vocabulary. When I give my word that I will do something, then I 'ought' to do it. When I claim a right then I 'should' acknowledge a responsibility. This is all part of building trust. Today many of us prefer to operate in a paradigm of needs, compassion, support rather than strict rules and regulations but there are some precepts such as honesty and justice and non-violence to which we must surely aspire.

Precepts such as 'Tell the truth', ' Eschew violence', 'Keep your word', are matters of will-power. However, although Christ and other spiritual leaders have enjoined us to 'Love one another' this is not something which can be achieved by the will alone. We can be kind and compassionate to each other but Love in its fullest sense is beyond this. This has been one of the primary puzzles of my life and I return to it later in the chapter on 'Love'.

Time

Angelus Silesius said, 'The soul has two eyes. One looks at time passing and the other sends forth its gaze into eternity.' This concept of eternity is difficult. Our mind is not big enough yet to comprehend it. Yet this may hold the key to so many other things which we do not understand. Maybe we can approach this awareness in meditation? We can also ask, 'How is it that we can have intuition about the future?' Maybe it is this incomprehensible element in Time which holds the key to resurrection and 'life after death'?

Affirming past, present and future

In the millennium year we held an exploration week at a retreat house on the Isle of Skye. One evening we sat by the log fire, each with a length of wool, and talked about the significant events which had happened in our lives (all of that past time being, of course, in the last millennium). We tied a knot in our yarn for each event. We then went on to think of the significant events in the history of humanity since the beginning of the world and again tied a knot for each. At the end of the evening we took these lengths of knotted yarn and tied them into a continuous circle, and the following morning we spread this out beside the rolling northern sea. As we stood inside this circle, we felt enclosed by the past and then, as we stepped backwards outside the circle, we felt the opportunities of the new millennium - and we danced.

Transpersonal Experience / Transforming Power

Many of us have experienced at some time a sense of something beyond our present existence - sometimes called a 'transpersonal experience'.

In order to tap into this we often ask, 'What makes your heart sing?' or 'What makes you fully alive?' The kind of peak experiences which women relate describe feelings of peace, energy, joy, oneness with all creation, love, timelessness, ecstasy and transcendence - such as may have caught them unawares when out in the mountains ('a sense of something far more deeply interfused') or by the sea, in the stillness of the countryside or even just waiting for a bus. This sometimes seems to happen when the whole being is integrated and focussed on something of beauty, but most of us are unable to invoke it deliberately and it may manifest in a variety of ways.

Such an experience often lasts for just a few moments but it can last for much longer. I have shared with women for whom it has been an ongoing experience of immense energising love in which there is an impetus to help and relate to everyone we meet. It may be described in different ways, but a major experience of this kind transforms lives. Perhaps it was this which Buddha experienced when he spoke of his 'Enlightenment'. Perhaps it was experienced by Jesus during his forty-eight days in the wilderness (especially when coupled with the expectation of Messiahship which had been thrust on him since birth and with the spiritual preparation which this entailed). Such an experience would explain how he came to be the special person he was - a man who could give us the sermon on the mount and all his teachings of love and peace.

But many of us experience lesser versions of this, some perhaps only lasting a few seconds. How would we want to try and explain it?

I refer to my own transpersonal experiences in 'My Story' as being one of the motives for writing this book. Very often someone telling of such an experience will say, 'I have never told anyone about this before'. In a sense, it feels sacred and we guard it like a tender plant, but having now shared my own experience with others many times, and realising that it was known by mystics in the past, I realise that it could be a phenomenon of great significance and one which needs much further exploration. It also often evokes the recollection of a similar experience from someone else.

I used to think that such a transpersonal experience could not be deliberately evoked - that it always came unawares. Now I am not so sure. It is not likely to be found by someone who is just looking for a 'spiritual experience'. But if someone is wanting to contribute from such a state of being to their community, then it would be a good preparation to practise a spiritual discipline on a regular basis for about six months in order to integrate body and mind - left and right brain. Then, relaxing in deep awareness and wonder in a place of beauty with a completely open mind and lack of expectation might evoke such an experience.

Recalling such a state of being can be a focus for meditation or finding inner strength.

In the Christian context this would be referred to as 'The Gift of Grace' or 'The Pentecostal experience'. For some in the Pentecostal tradition this can be a very frequent experience giving intense liberation and joy. But it manifests in many ways and can often be the source of a longer lasting, outflowing, energising love. On the other hand it may manifest in behaviour which we do not understand.

Such phenomenon may also be linked with 'Transforming Power' which is recognised in the 'Twelve Step Programme' for Alcoholics Anonymous and in 'Alternatives to Violence' workshops which I referred to briefly in the chapter on 'Circle'. Even outside the workshop, at times of crisis someone may experience an unusual expansion of their capabilities or the courage to face a threatening situation.

It reminds us that 'there is more to life than those things we can touch or see' and in any consideration of 'Spirituality', we need to be aware of this. Some might want to call it 'God' - others not.

I wonder whether such experience might also relate to Christ's promise of 'life in abundance'?

Silence

Our Western tradition is so full of words. But we are increasingly understanding the value of silence. This is something which we can all share whatever our belief or lack of it. We begin our mornings at the Grange with half an hour of shared silence. This may be an opportunity for silent prayer or meditation.

Prayer

Prayer in the past has often been understood in terms of requesting something from a higher power, whether for ourselves or for others. It has often been a 'shopping list' of requests or cries for help and guidance. For many Christians today there has been a shift from the status of creature (eg, 'Help me', 'Save me', 'Forgive me') to that of co-creator - as with St Francis ('Make me an instrument of your peace'). Whether we believe in God or not, it can be a spontaneous longing for something, a well-wishing for another. A healer may open herself to a higher energy with a prayer.

Imaginatively, we can create a sense of the presence of something beyond our present understanding in wonder and gratitude, and in this light seek guidance. I am not suggesting that we imagine something unreal or untrue, but simply that we are still too small and do not understand enough. We need to use our powers of imagination and experience to bring such an intuitive awareness into present reality. In such an awareness we find a higher perspective and a healing peace.

When praying for another person we may bring the person prayed for into the light (or into the presence of a benign energy) and surround them with love. There seems evidence that such prayer can have a healing effect, creating a loving connection with the person concerned which can be life-enhancing if not life-giving There is so much we do not know about the power of the mind, about any other power at present beyond our comprehension and about other powers which may emerge with our future evolution. We may also use symbols in intercession, as I explain further on.

Many women belong to a prayer network and have a special time of day for personal prayer. In extreme old age when it may become impossible even to pray, then the person may herself become the focus of prayer by others which can itself be valuable in bringing group cohesion which might more helpfully be called 'love'.

Prayer groups usually include a time for intercession and are otherwise mainly based on meditation.

Meditation
We spoke of this briefly during our 'Resource Group' sessions at St James'. This is a word with different meanings for different

people. For some, it may mean thinking around a given text or topic. For others, it may mean the contemplation of something beautiful such as a flower or a flame. This indeed can be one of the gateways to the silence of what I shall call Meditation with a capital 'M'.

For me Meditation means relaxing completely, clearing the mind in total awareness - being in the presence of the Divine - touching the intuitive and the creative within. It is a state of being which can be scientifically identified as the brain moves into alpha rhythm.

Paradoxically, Meditation is the simplest thing in the world - I can just let go and relax into wonder. Yet at the same time, as a regular discipline, it takes practice and does not come easily. The first step may be a form of contemplation in which the focus is held on a beautiful object such as a flower or a candle flame - or on awareness of breathing, learning how to relax and allow the mind to become still. Some people like to start with a mantra. A Christian one could be repetition of 'Maranatha' (Come Lord Jesus) or 'Aum' (signifying past present and future in NOW). 'Aum' can be a powerful group meditation as the word ends in a hum creating a continuous sound as each voice brings a different note together, blending in harmony without losing each distinctive tone. Personally, having found that I could 'stop the conversation inside', I was loathe to fill my mind with mantra words and for me the best entry is simply to visualise light on water. I find that it helps to spend the previous twenty minutes in yoga practice so that the balance and relaxation of the body can be reflected in the mind, but we are all different and the only way to find out what is best for you is to keep practising. A regular daily practice can bring about an inner peace which will gradually extend into the rest of life.

When you surrender to what is, and so become fully present, the past ceases to have any power. The realm of Being, which had been obscured by the mind, then opens up. Suddenly a great stillness arises within you, an unfathomable sense of place.

And within that place, there is great joy. And within that joy
there is love. And at the innermost core, there is the sacred,
the immeasurable, that which cannot be named.

Eckhart Tolle

But sometimes the first attempt to relax may allow all sorts of events which have been suppressed in the mind to come to the surface so that the experience is far from peaceful. It may be necessary to find a guide to help with these problems.

There are numerous books of guidance and many groups these days who will instruct and encourage. A group Meditation is often easier and more powerful than Meditating alone.

It may also be able to create peacefulness in the surrounding area. There is evidence from those who practise Transcendental Meditation (TM) that when they Meditate together in a group, violence in the immediate environment diminishes significantly. This has been witnessed in areas of conflict and in prisons.

Guided Meditation is different again (and might perhaps be better called 'Guided Visualisation') as it involves imagining oneself in a different place - often on a journey. It can be used to explore the unconscious and in this case the journey usually involves meeting a wise person and asking him/her a question. The reply probably comes from deep in the unconscious. The experience is usually discussed afterwards. Another kind of Guided Visualisation, however, is simply to induce relaxation and serenity, in which case the state of mind is preserved afterwards without discussion.

There is a kind of guided visualisation which gives the opportunity to imagine a journey into the future and create the serene and joyous mindset of someone at that time. In this case there needs to be no discussion afterwards but simply a retention of stillness and silence.

Mindfulness

Thich Nat Hanh teaches 'Mindfulness' - total focus on what is happening and what we are doing in the present. This induces a meditative state and an awareness of the present moment - the reality of NOW. However, concentration on an occupation such as knitting, swimming or walking can also free the mind for creative activity. Concentrating on washing-up may bring me to the immediacy of the present moment and into a state of Meditation, but allowing this activity to take up only the surface energies of my mind may instead enable me to create a poem or letter. Both have value. Both remind us to observe how our mind is occupied.

Physical basis

There is increasing awareness of how mind, body and spirit are connected to each other so that our state of mind and spirit can be affected by the body and vice-versa.

Therapies

On our exploration weekends at the Grange, various therapies are available from Ali - a trained therapist in reflexology, aromatherapy, reiki and Indian head massage. Many of the women who come on these weekends are also therapists. In the last fifty years or more a huge range of new therapies have surfaced. Although this is usually combined with the philosophy that the patient should take responsibility herself for her own health, it also brings awareness of how physical treatment from another can be helpful and how such therapies can complement the traditional medical care provided by doctors and nurses. Such an emergence of new treatments may relate to an increasing sensitivity (or as some would say a 'higher vibrational level'). Implicit in all of them is the importance of a caring relationship and good attention, which can be healing in itself.

Yoga and Tai Chi, etc. (see also Appendix)
Physical discipline in relation to the spiritual path is something which is more widely recognised in the East. In the West it has often been assumed in the past that the mind /spirit was separate from a body/'the flesh'. The old male Christian theologians used to consider the body as an enemy which had to be kept under control (rather like trying to control a donkey). Now there is increasing recognition of the body as the temple of the spirit - it is only as we learn to understand and care for our bodies that our minds and spirits can function properly.

Yehudi Menuhin pointed out that before he played his violin, he needed to tune it up or it would be incapable of producing music, and in the same way he tuned up his body with yoga every day. We in the West have much to learn from the Chinese people who practise Tai Chi in their parks and open spaces every morning. Yoga and Tai Chi are more specifically spiritual physical traditions in the way they can produce integration, balance, and inner stillness, but walking or swimming on a regular basis can have some of the same effect and can be a good preparation for Meditation or, in fact, be a time of Meditation in themselves.

Some of us are conscious of the chakra system - the seven energy points from the base of the spine to the crown of the head. Each relates to a different aspect of life, and by yoga posture and breathing we can bring them into balance.

Dance
Dancing is a way of bringing mind, body and spirit into unity. My own experience recently has been mainly with circle dance in which many people find harmony, both within the individual and between members of the dancing group. These are mostly very ancient simple dances, some perhaps even pre-dating speech. There are also others which have been choreographed for modern music such as the Taize chants or folk song. The dances can be symbolic, celebratory, meditational, grieving or just fun.

Anthony de Mello tells the story of a rabbi who visited a village in Russia where they all expected him to speak words of great wisdom; instead, he slowly began to hum and then to dance, inviting everyone to join with him. Finally he sat down and said, "Now I hope you have the answer to all your questions."

Moving meditation

Maggie and Eileen, who came to our explorations, had devised their own movements as a morning Meditation. I am always amazed how beautiful a woman looks when she is totally focussed on something like this and moving in a way which has become a part of her life. Her whole being radiates an inner beauty. The movements are symbolic gestures. Eileen moves to the music of Bach's Air on a G string.

Food and Fasting

We know that what we eat and drink not only affects our general well-being but indirectly affects our behaviour. Our food and drink also has relevance in the spiritual context. I do not claim to be vegetarian myself, although I would like to be and admire those who are. There are ethical and nutritional reasons for this. As long ago as 1971, Frances Moore Lappe[20] pointed out that sixteen pounds of grain and soy is reduced by the average bullock into one pound of steak on our plates. This cannot be the best way of using the world's resources!

Apart from this, I could not myself kill an animal for meat, so why should I expect anyone else to do this? There are anecdotal evidence that a vegetarian diet enables increased bodily suppleness and awareness as well as reducing aggressive behaviour, and I'm sure that research is ongoing. It has also been suggested that the consumption of battery-reared animals leads to depression - a state of mind being conveyed from the animal to the consumer. Again, only research will provide evidence. Some yogis claim that onions and garlic are too stimulating and omit them from their diet.

Many abstain from alcohol as I do myself. This is partly because of the danger of addiction (and to give moral support to those who are coming off such an addiction) but alcohol also clouds the natural clarity of the senses. Total abstinence as a prerequisite of spiritual growth is one of the things which we might learn from our Muslim friends. More consideration is given to this subject in the section on 'Meals' in the 'Rhythms of the Day' later in this chapter.

Then there is fasting. I don't have a wide experience of this, although I learnt from my Muslim friends how much Ramadan meant to them - especially the extra time which they spent in prayer and study of sacred texts. For some years I fasted for a whole day each week during Lent (the Christian fasting period when it is traditional to give up some favourite food such as chocolate) but realised that I didn't really find it very difficult and in fact I was simply demonstrating to myself my own will-power. Like my Muslim friends, I spent extra time reading sacred texts, relevant books and poetry (although on a more wide-ranging basis than them). Such reading made the fast far more meaningful and, certainly, lack of food gave a kind of inner space (as, it seems, does living on small quantities of bread and honey). I understand from friends' experience that longer fasting can have a deeper spiritual relevance which I have not yet discovered.

Celibacy

This is a spiritual discipline which has a somewhat different practice in the East. In the West it is simply seen as a form of denial and is usually a life-long commitment. (We need to question the lifelong commitment to celibacy undertaken by those devoting their life to God, before they have had much life experience.) In parts of the East, and especially combined with the yoga discipline, it is regarded as a positive way of living, maybe just for short periods, which will increase spiritual awareness and will encourage other forms of expressing love. Both sexuality and celibacy are sacred and each way of living has its own value.

Pilgrimage

Another way of combining the physical and the spiritual is to go on a pilgrimage. This need not be a major expedition; it can take place simply in one day, as when a group in Rugby set off on an Interfaith pilgrimage around the various places of worship in the town. This was a way of sharing their common humanity and understanding more about each other's faiths.

The final destination of the pilgrimage varies. In England some of the favourite places are the shrine at Walsingham, Canterbury cathedral, the chalice well in Glastonbury and Holy Island off the north-east coast. A long-standing European pilgrimage is that of the Camino path to Santiago de Compostello. For Muslims the most obvious pilgrimage is to Mecca.

My husband and I went walking up the pilgrimage trail of Sri Pada in Sri Lanka, the high mountain where the huge footprint of Buddha is said to be imprinted in the rock on the top. Although the experience at the top was memorable, as the dawn sunlight outlined the shape of the mountain on a bank of cloud, the part I remember best was the encounter with fellow pilgrims going up and down and I vividly recall our chat with members of the Kandy fire brigade on what may have been their annual outing.

I have also been on pilgrimage with my daughter in India on the trail to Kedarnath (Shiva's sacred home), starting by bus from Rishikesh and then the next day walking from Gaurikund up the beautiful valley of the river Alaknanda, one of the tributaries of the Ganges, and finally on horseback to a golden roofed temple near the head of the valley. At this point we were just above the snow line. Although I was invited into the temple, my Western mindset could not resonate with the ceremonies going on inside, where, in the smoky half light, plates of rice and other food were being wafted in offering. However, outside, the sheer beauty of the snowy peaks, the radiant skies and the rushing clear water was uplifting. Another essential part of the experience was the way in which all pilgrims greeted each other going up and coming down: "Jai Kedarnath". In fact, it is not the destination but the experience of the journey itself which is valuable, as encapsulated in the poem 'Ithaka' by C. P. Cavafy:

When you set out for Ithaka
ask that your way be long, full of adventure,
full of instruction . . .

Have Ithaka always in your mind.
Your arrival there is what
you are destined for.
But don't in the least hurry the journey.
Better it last for years
so that when you reach the island
you are old,
rich with all you gained on the way,
not expecting Ithaka to give you wealth.
Ithaka gave you a splendid journey.
Without her you would not have set out.
She hasn't anything else to give you.

Symbols

Symbols can be a more potent means of expression when words fail us. One way of finding a deeper significance in life is by marking events with a ceremony or rite of passage. A symbolic ceremony can anchor an event deep within and it can manifest its meaning in our society. We need to create such ceremonies as a way of bringing an event into full reality and recognition. Historically the ancient faiths have provided us with ceremonies mainly concerned with birth, marriage and death. However, in our increasingly multicultural society it is good to have ceremonies which we can share and rites of passage which can affirm other events in life as well. There can be other ceremonies, for example for a girl's first period, for starting a job, for retirement, losing a job, moving house and above all perhaps moving into the second half of life after the menopause. Older women are in an ideal position to co-create and enable the creation of such ceremonies and rituals.

Different faiths have adopted icons to express the central meaning of their beliefs. For us today one of the central icons could be the Tree of Life. I repeat what I said in the Introduction as this seems of vital importance. In the mythology of the three great Western religions (Christianity, Judaism and Islam) the story of the Garden of Eden at the beginning of the world contains two trees. The second tree was the Tree of Life (perhaps symbolising spiritual growth) but it is interesting how this has been largely ignored over the centuries while all the focus has been on the forbidden Tree of Knowledge. Our knowledge has now grown from apple pies and cider to Apple Mac and cyberspace and it is still growing - so it is high time that we paid attention to the second tree. Christ said, "I came that ye might have life and that ye might have it more abundantly," but priests who followed him spoke more of death than of life, symbolising suffering and death in the symbol of the cross.

The symbol of a seed or an egg, both containing huge potential for a life which is not even hinted at in the exterior appearance could also be valuable symbols today.

The Four Elements

In the ancient world our ancestors were conscious of the four elements - Earth, Water, Fire and Air. Windows of awareness can be opened by the opportunity to resonate with such symbols. Many of our groups have used them in different ways.

In one of our circle dance weekends, June arranged the four elements each in different corners of the room. Objects such as plants, flowers and stones represented Earth; a bowl of water was in the next corner; lit candles on a table covered in a red and gold cloth in the third corner represented Fire; and feathers in the last corner represented Air (we might perhaps have used incense). We were each asked to spend some time in each corner and just allow the elements to resonate with us how they might. On this particular weekend, whilst in the Earth corner, I found myself thinking of my father and grandfather's family, as my ancestors on that side of the family were mostly farmers. In the corner with the bowl of water I resonated with my mother's family who were associated with the river as boat builders. In the corner full of candles I remembered the people in my life who had inspired me, and in the final corner - Air - the unknown future. On other occasions the elements have been meaningful in other ways.

It is worth remembering that these four elements are the inanimate components of our world. In order to have a whole representation we need to include the concept of life using such symbols as an egg, a living flower or an acorn.

The Use of Symbols in Other Ceremonies

I refer in my story to the sessions 'Beyond Words' which were held in the tower room at St James' church, Piccadilly, in London in 1985. These sessions explored the use of symbols and created seeds which later developed at the Grange and elsewhere. In London we had weekly sessions. Each week we explored symbols for a different subject, beginning with thanksgiving, then forgiveness and reconciliation, followed by intercession and dedication. After this we made or produced symbols to mark each major transition of a woman's life. Sometimes these were later developed into ceremonies at the Grange or elsewhere. I should like to follow them through as we experienced them and also talk about ceremonies devised by others. In each case I begin by describing our session in London.

Thanksgiving

We focussed on gratitude. We brought flowers, but some took a square of green velvet and stuck on it a gold star for each of the people in their lives to whom they wanted to give special thanks. At the Grange this developed into a ceremony which usually takes place on the third evening of our exploration weekend; a celebration of women who have in some way inspired us. This can be a woman we have known in our childhood, whom we know now, a woman from history, or someone out there in the wider world - not necessarily a role model but just someone we admire and to whom we are grateful. This gives the opportunity to celebrate some of the unsung women who live lives of courage, compassion, imagination and dedication and to focus on some of the qualities which we admire. Very often mothers or grandmothers or teachers are chosen - sometimes friends, as well as women who have made their mark in the world for a variety of reasons. During the afternoon we pick a flower to represent the woman we wish to celebrate. In the evening we hold this flower and tell something about the woman represented, before putting it in a bowl of leaves around the central candle. We then all honour her by saying her name and bowing our heads in a gesture of 'namaste'. Such tributes are interspersed with circle dancing.

Forgiveness and reconciliation

When we came to consider forgiveness we had a bowl of cherries and each took one. Having savoured the appearance, the smell and the taste, we ate it, finding the hard stone in the middle which we related to some hurt or resentment or even enmity. We thought about how such a situation had come about and about the person we wanted to forgive. Then we each buried our stone in a bowl of soil with the prayer that it would be transformed and grow up into something beautiful. Forgiving someone through prayer *in absentia* may be the first step in a true healing. These concepts relate very closely to guilt which (like fear) can be a huge blockage to liberation into a more abundant life. Traditional Christians find forgiveness in Christ's sacrifice on the cross (although some compound their guilt by thinking that what they have done has increased his agony). For those who can no longer believe this we need to evolve some ceremony of forgiveness, acceptance and love from the supporting community . . . from the cosmic Christ within each one of us. It is difficult, and so far we have not come up with any very effective ceremony except a washing of each other's hands or feet. The 'truth and reconciliation' procedures which have evolved in Mozambique, South Africa and Ireland can surely show us the way.

Intercession

We talked of the need to eliminate anxiety and urgency from intercession, concentrating on the whole person rather than on the disease. We recognised that death was a natural part of the life cycle and that we were not praying for any definite outcome, but simply holding that person in love. We spoke of lighting a candle for someone and knowing that the flame would go on burning after we had left. To symbolise the process of casting a person on the supporting love of a higher power, we placed a flower on water as we said a name and then allowed healing to flow through us. At the Grange we have not developed this any further. When we blow out the candle at the end of a session, however, we sometimes say the names of those to whom we would wish the light to be sent in blessing.

Dedication

We acknowledged that the dictionary definition of dedication is 'to set apart'. We thought this could be true of a building but for most people an involvement with life would be an integral part of any dedication. We placed a central candle in a bowl of water from which we each lit our own candle. Holding the candle in one hand, symbolising inspiration and love, we placed the other hand in the water of life as a gesture of commitment. We noted the resemblance of this to the alchemical circle of the four elements - Earth, Water, Fire and Air. It is often too easy to read *about* theology, or theories of good and evil, or the work of other people, rather than daring to plunge into life itself and explore.

At the Grange we have incorporated a dedication ceremony with milk and honey into our closing liturgy. I describe this later under 'Closure'.

Symbols and Ceremonies to Mark a Woman's Life Cycle

Again I start by describing our experience in the tower room at St James' in 1985.

Birth

For this session the various symbolic objects placed on the table were: a young living plant which would flower and fruit, a candle in a star holder, a pink crystal egg, a wooden ring, positive and negative flexes coming to a bulb holder, a red handkerchief symbolising blood, a cockle-shell filled with water, a rosebud, a bursting ear of corn, the opening shell of an avocado. But we still felt that these symbols did not express the pain, the struggle, the mess, the inevitability, the vulnerability of this time and the awareness of death in life. We listened to a recording of the sea, remembering that all life came from the sea and noting the similarity of birth contractions to the waves.

We imagined ourselves as proverbial fairy godmothers who each gave gifts to the newborn child. We all gave love and the emotional security which goes with it - and then hope. We recognised that both of these we could give ourselves. After this we wanted the baby to have joy and laughter, courage and understanding.

Most religions have ceremonies to welcome the child into their faith. However, before this all children need to be welcomed into the world.

Rosemary recently created a 'Welcome to the World' ceremony for her new grandson, Zak. She invited family and friends into her home, she made a cake and invited anyone who so wished to give a reading or say a prayer. Her grandchild was welcomed and the parents given support in what was a very pleasant social and yet sacred occasion.

Menarche (a girl's first period)

This is one of the most important events in a girl's life, yet our society gives it no recognition. Although the dictionaries we consulted had not mentioned the word 'menarche' the Oxford dictionary helpfully pointed out that the menstrual element was a *'vital compound to transform base metal into gold'*. Perhaps symbolic in itself?

Most tribes have an initiation ceremony for children, coming into the status of adulthood. Often this can be primitive and painful, and not something we would wish to emulate, but the lack of any such ceremony in our own society may be one of the causes of so much youthful turbulence and delinquency.

Symbols of 'menarche' produced in our first sessions were: the moon, a picture of the Grail, of blood within the womb, a shell-covered box with a red lining containing a linking chain of gold leaves and a silver snake symbolising not only the sanctity of wisdom and health but the sacredness of sexuality.

At the Grange we have talked about devising a ceremony

which affirms the qualities of the young person involved, initiates them into adult responsibility and assures a circle of older women who can give support and encouragement in times of need. Now that a girl's first period may happen at such a young age, we have considered it better to have such a ceremony later, becoming a woman in the context of family and society.

Frederica Chapman with her daughter, Hilary, evolved a lovely ceremony around the time when her daughter first experienced menstruation. She has written about it in a book called *A Girl's Gateway to Womanhood* with suggestions how this can be planned. To other mothers she says:

Rather than look to puberty as a predictable time for your daughter to rebel and find herself in trouble, you could look to the relationship you have developed with her up to now, and trust that it will shift, expand and grow. Yes, she needs space in which to discover herself, but with your help and permission she could make her necessary discoveries and changes in a flowing manner. Continuing to believe in your child's goodness and ability to make positive choices will encourage her to do so. She needs your faith, she needs your boundaries and she needs your willingness to step back.

Addressing her daughter she says:

You are consciously participating in your life story. The celebration marks an ending and a beginning. It celebrates who you have become and who you are becoming. I believe that you will find joy in marking this event as you will find joy in welcoming growth all your life through.

Mother and daughter planned the ceremony about three months in advance. Hilary's main skills were in pottery and dance, so she decided that she would prepare a piece of pottery and a dance for the occasion; she also chose two of her mother's friends to act as her mentors. During the three-month period leading up to the ceremony, she spent a little time with each of these friends on several occasions. This gave the opportunity for getting to know each other on a basis of trust. When the day came, Hilary's friends and her mother's friends were all invited to see the pottery and watch the dance and the girl stepped through an arch of greenery to be embraced by them all and to share a meal together. Thereafter these mentors would be available for her. I recommend that you obtain the book[21] and read it for yourself because there is much more than this in it.

In a book called *The Wise Wound* (by Penelope Shuttle and Peter Redgrove), the writers point out that instead of being called 'The Curse' (as my generation used to call it), menstruation should be called the 'Woman's Friend'(as it is in many languages) because for those who are in tune with their bodies and with the rhythm of the cycle there is immense creativity and intuitive knowledge in the period of the paramenstrum (ie, four days before bleeding begins and the first four days of bleeding). This is a time when a woman needs to go within and discover the wealth of spiritual creativity although it can be a bad time for those who are not in tune (and of course there may be medical reasons for pain at this time). Some of us confirmed the creative and energising aspect of the paramenstrum from our own experience.

We spoke of the creativity of chaste relationships as well as the sacredness of physical sexuality.

Vocation

When considering this in our early sessions we thought that sometimes a vocation was just for the chosen few. Yet every single person makes up the fabric of life and each interacts with the rest. Someone suggested that a maypole dance could symbolise the way we together weave our pattern of life, each having our own coloured ribbon. We felt it was important not to think in terms of career or job. Just because a person is unemployed, this does not mean that she is useless. Her value in human terms does not depend on money, although she may be forced into taking a job which she feels is not right for her or may be unable to find work at all.

We recognised that vocation was not static, but might change as life went on.

We affirmed each other's vocation and dedication by pouring milk and honey (to demonstrate God's overflowing goodness and love) into our neighbour's bowl with the words 'May the spirit of love grow within you'. Then, holding coloured ribbons (which were anchored beneath a central pot containing a cross transforming into the Tree of Life) we would like to have danced our maypole dance had space allowed. Instead we read a poem by D. H. Lawrence beginning 'Not I, but the wind that blows through me' and the prayer of St Francis: 'Make me an instrument of your peace'. This is a good example of symbolic overload!

At the Grange we have often considered how to find vocation. In the past it was often assumed that this would be hard and difficult and go against the grain. If we start from this assumption a vocation may well end in martyrdom and will probably be very tiresome for the person involved and everyone else. A quotation from Findhorn suggests:

> *Don't ask what the world needs*
> *Ask what makes you alive*
> *And then go and do it!*
> *Because what the world needs is*
> *People who are truly alive.*

I suspect that we may probably want to bring some of the other needs of the world into the equation somewhere, but this is a good starting point.

Marriage

Some would say that marriage will soon be a thing of the past, but as a basis for bringing up healthy and secure children we have not yet found a better alternative. For all sorts of practical reasons it is easier for two people to create a secure environment.

During the early session in London we talked too much, but also produced a most beautiful nest with evergreen sprays, thistles, many other symbolic flowers and honeysuckle trailing out into the world!

I realised later that this is a symbol of a home rather than of marriage. Perhaps this is significant. Of course for many there is no ambition to bring up a family. The intention is simply to give each other love and support. Both types of marriage may spring from the same experience of 'falling in love', but the couple who are planning to create a new generation of human beings have a far greater challenge and commitment. So many today are afraid of commitment. Arranged marriages are condemned in the west and it is true that those made on the basis of commercial or political interests are rarely a success. However, there are also families in other parts of the world where the parents plan their children's marriages (with their agreement) on the basis of compatibility and shared values, which is surely a sound basis for a home where children are to be reared. Both partners then make a conscious effort to generate love by a deep level sharing and caring (as we do in circle). Some of the happiest marriages are formed in this way.

Increasingly the young are devising their own rituals for wedding ceremonies, particularly if they feel uncomfortable with a church ceremony but still want more spiritual or symbolic input than a registry office usually offers. Our younger daughter Rosie and her partner Jon wanted to have their wedding at the Grange and decided to use a Celtic theme. As the Grange was not licensed for wedding ceremonies, they had a civil ceremony in London a few days before which gave them the opportunity to have some space for themselves. Then on the day of the wedding there were Morris dancers in the garden while the guests assembled. Rosie had left home long ago so it would have made no sense for her father to 'give her away' as in the traditional wedding service. She wore a beautiful white brocade dress with gold collar as she and Jon walked across the meadow, with bridesmaid following, on to the front lawn of the house and the guests gathered round in a circle. The ceremony had been specially written for this occasion. It was based on some old Celtic traditions and in true Celtic spirit borrowed features from other cultures and parts of the world. The celebrant Helen, who was Rosie's godmother, greeted them and the guests. After a reading, Jon and Rosie drank mead from a silver cup. This was followed by the Celtic handfasting ceremony in which the joined hands were bound by a red ribbon to make a dual circle that has come to represent infinity and perfect union. The couple then turned in a clockwise direction and made their commitment to each other. Two friends gave readings and then rings were exchanged. It was set in the context of family history by signing their names in the old Bible which had belonged to Rosie's great, great, grandmother. The ceremony ended with a blessing. Then Helen invited us all to join in a Zimbabwean handshake by which everyone greets everyone else. After the meal (which all the family had prepared - including a spit roast over a bonfire), and songs from the guests, we all joined in Celtic (in this case, Scottish) dancing.

The civil ceremony for two people of the same gender is an interesting new development and again can be set in a symbolic context.

Pregnancy

In our session at St James', we meditated on a seed, thinking of all the potential growth. We wanted to listen to the mother's heart beat (at first at one with the child but then differentiating), but the carefully prepared cassette could not be used because of a fuse in the tape recorder! However, we read the poem which should have accompanied this of a mother to her unborn child, recognising that in the oneness of their physical life there must also be a oneness of thought and emotion. We realised from this that it is very important for a woman to choose carefully what occupies her thought and emotions during this time. Sheelagh suggested that a woman's pregnancy might be celebrated as a rite of passage by family and friends so that support could be given at an earlier stage - however, most thought that pregnancy was a joyful secret which in the early stages couples might not want to share. It was also pointed out that it was not always a joyful time at all. For others a much longed for child may seem to be beyond possibility. However those who discover the joy of new life will want to celebrate and give thanks.

Menopause

Those of us exploring 'Beyond Words' (our group at St James') suggested that the most peaceful cultures in the past were run by wise women. We also recognised that now, for the first time in the history of the world, older women had health, education and longevity, with the opportunity to explore new paths and develop a spirituality in touch with nature and the reality of our human condition. For symbols we each chose a fruit, appreciating its colour, texture and smell, noticing the difference between them and the seeds or stone containing the potential for future growth

At the Grange some told us of a 'croning' ceremony in which they had been crowned as a wise woman. For others a sixtieth birthday celebration had been their rite of passage. It can be a creative and affirming experience to devise such a ceremony with a group of friends. Several ceremonies have been created over the years in our exploration sessions. For Clare's sixtieth birthday we began with a simple circle dance and then the 'under sixties' stood in a double row joining their upraised hands to make arches under which Clare passed before being welcomed into the circle of 'over sixties' and being given a symbolic gift by the eldest. She then sat in the middle of the circle while we all danced a celebration dance round her. This was a simple Israeli circle dance, Nigun Atik, which is used to celebrate a bridal couple or someone's birthday. On other occasions the ceremony has involved the symbolic lighting of a candle or crowning with a wreath of flowers.

During a 'Rites of Passage' workshop that we held soon after we arrived at the Grange, Jeanie and I moved into the 'Second Half of Life'. We were part of a circle dancing to the music of Pachelbel - the dance of three steps forward and one step in (an adaptation of the Crusaders' dance) which we now associate with awareness of the menstrual cycle. At an agreed moment we moved from the moving circle into the middle, which was intended to symbolise that we would be within the protection of the younger women and at the same time be in a central position as - eventually - possible disseminators of wisdom! In fact this was too simplistic. The period after the menopause, as we enter the second half of life, has a different rhythm and potential from that of both earlier and later life and at this stage there is no need for protection from the younger women (possibly the other way round). However, devising such ceremonies together not only brings out the creativity of all concerned but also can affirm the value of this period of life. Some women regard coming to one of our weekends as a rite of passage in itself!

Death

In our first session at St James' we listened to music from *Fauré's Requiem* and later, a Gregorian chant. Our symbol was a flower head fallen from its stalk and Jean's poem about falling petals.

We spoke of living life in awareness of death and how that would ensure that we 'did our washing up as we went along', giving a new freedom in relationships. We can only live life to the full when we have come to terms with our own mortality. Whether we believe in a life hereafter, in reincarnation, or simply that time is an illusion and that life happens in a much wider perspective of eternity, death as an end to life as we know it is inevitable. Its prospect can be life enhancing. Sometimes the awareness comes from a near-death experience or from the death of someone who is close to us, it may come in a church-yard or during a funeral service - perhaps even through some event on television.

Beyond death - Beyond Time

Life after death is usually understood in linear time. Yet we are now able to understand it in the context of being outside time. I am indebted to Philip Sheppard for expressing this more clearly than I have been able to do:

It is a paradigm shift from entities to relationship. The fundamental unit of existence is a loving relationship. God is not a solitary being; God is a loving relationship. God exists in the eternal now where time does not exist. This is the innermost centre of all that is. This is the source from which everything emerges in the beginning and the destination to which everything returns in the end. Everything is an outward expression of inner love. Everything is attracted back to the centre from which it came. This centre can be found in the depths of every human heart, where God is eternally at home. This outward inward journey is the pilgrimage of life.

To imagine time as a straight line is like imagining that the world is flat. It is a useful approximation as long as you are not too adventurous. Linear time corresponds to the horizontal axis of a cartesian co-ordinate system. It belongs with the individualistic 'I think therefore I am' paradigm.

As we become more aware of the power and diversity of love we begin to see the world in a different way, where relationship and community are of prime importance, and at the same time we become more aware of different aspects of time.

This awareness of being outside time is available to everyone through mystical experience of oneness (as described earlier). It can be accessed through the silence of meditation.For some who have lived solitary lives it may be a first experience of love while for others it may primarily be an awareness of those whom they have loved during life.

At the Grange we have sometimes found that women have come with a fear of death. One had been diagnosed with cancer and although, after treatment, she had been declared clear, she was still living in the fear which this news had brought her. Another saw her mother sitting on the edge of the sofa terrified of dying and wanted to be able to help her, as well as finding peace of mind for herself.

Fear of death, like any other fear, can be limiting, if not paralysing. What is this fear? Is it fear of the possible pain of the dying process rather than death itself? Is it fear of what may lie beyond? Or simply fear of the unknown? Occasionally women have overcome their fear during the weekend. Sometimes they have found some seeds of hope in the experience of others.

One woman, whom I will call Una, had not told us about her fear of death. It was while we were doing an exercise in recalling any transpersonal experience that she remembered a time when she had been on her own out in the country beside an old stone circle. As she looked at the sunlight on the stones she was suddenly aware of a much bigger dimension, of being at one with the universe, finding peace and joy and an overflowing love for everyone and everything. She had never mentioned it to anyone before and had almost forgotten it. But as she now recalled it and affirmed it, she suddenly found that her fear of death had gone.

Someone else whom I will call Elspeth described the beautiful death of her mother who had loved singing. She and her mother sang all their favourite songs together as she was dying.

Perhaps most importantly we need to 'leave our house in order', to get rid of the clutter, make provision for those who may depend on us, making sure that we are in a state of reconciliation with all those we love. Sometimes it can be helpful to write farewell letters. Stephanie Sorrell has written a poem:

If one day you find me gone
And no longer see my form
Walking through the door
As you remember,

Look for me in skies
Painted turquoise with the day,
In stars that make the heavens shine,
In the scented flames of gorse
That crown the hills.
See me in the eyes of one you love,
Look for me in the quiet of your heart . . .

These days many people like to devise a ceremony for their own funeral. For some this means simply requesting hymns and readings. Others envisage something more elaborate such as a party with champagne and fireworks. Anne suggested that planning the funeral was really for friends to do as part of the grieving process and that maybe we were pre-empting them by presenting a complete blueprint. Someone else pointed out that the sort of service which she would like would not be acceptable to some of her relatives and this is difficult. Talking about it in advance can at least clarify the situation so that a last minute clash of intention is avoided and perhaps some adjustment is enabled.

These days most people want to have a ceremony of celebration, or thanksgiving for the life of the person who has died. Whatever form is used, perhaps the most essential part is a personal reminiscence and tribute. The Quaker service which allows anyone to stand up and speak can be a heart-warming experience and this kind of service can be introduced by anyone in a crematorium for friends and family.

One idea is to write a testament of those things in life which have been of most value to you: the high points, the growing points and what has made life worth living. This can be your own testament to life read out at the final ceremony. These days it is possible to put a final message on video. We know of someone who, in terminal cancer, not only planned her funeral service but booked and paid for the reception afterwards in a beautiful place where she wanted to be remembered.

I have vivid and treasured memories of a funeral for a young friend I will call Fran. She was a single mother whose son was about six years old and she died from a brain tumour. For some months beforehand, I had been taking her to a cancer support group and, at what turned out to be the last meeting we attended before her death, she suddenly stood up and said, "I want to dance." And she danced - with complete freedom, grace and abandon round the room. Her sister was the celebrant at her funeral in the local crematorium and invited all of us to say something or to recall memories. This gave the opportunity for many appreciations and for recalling the precious lovely moments of her dance. After this we returned to the house where there was a large cake in the shape of a butterfly and photograph albums on the table showing Fran's life. We circle-danced and sang, which enabled the children to join in and we later planted a tree in her memory.

At the time of death of a close relative we are at our most vulnerable and not in the best frame of mind to make instant decisions about ceremonies. So it is well worth giving some thought to this beforehand if the people themselves have not given directions. In our groups we have talked about the pros and cons of cremation versus burial and the merits of green burials. The *Natural Death Handbook* gives information about inexpensive or alternative ways of being despatched and how to organise your own funeral in practical terms.

There are volunteer funeral advisers too who can be contacted through Cruse (the bereavement charity) and who can ease the stress at the death of a loved one and help to provide the sort of arrangements which you really need. Perhaps in the future there may be 'Resource Groups' which can provide personal support.

Grieving is a long process and it can be good to have some

ceremony on the anniversary of a death. This could be just a small informal gathering of friends. It can include a visit to the grave or to the place where ashes are scattered, but above all it is a time for recalling memories of the person in life, the kind of person they were, and honouring what they loved and lived for.

How do we wish to die?

The medical profession aim to save life at all costs as this is part of their Hippocratic oath. However, medical technology has now outrun itself and there is the ability to prolong life long after any quality of life is over.

Some believe that suffering in this life may enable a better start in the life to come. Some claim that growth comes through suffering. Others, who feel that this life is all there is, want to preserve a good quality of life as far as possible to the end, particularly when pain may evoke harsh words to those whom we cherish the most. Is recourse to intensive care always the best solution to collapse? Very often it may be close relatives, rather than the patient herself, who cannot let go and want to prolong life. On the other hand there may be relatives with the opposite hope who have ulterior motives.

Today at least we have the option of 'Living Wills'. In these documents (obtainable from the Natural Death Centre) we can give guidance to our doctor and family about our wishes for artificially prolonging life - or not. This enables us in advance to refuse resuscitation on the basis of one of three levels of deterioration. Such a document may be a help to doctors and relatives but it does not have legal validity. Tragic deaths, particularly from motor neurone disease, in the past few years have brought this issue to a wider public.

It is a subject which urgently needs to be widely and openly discussed but this may only be possible in a climate of love and trust in which the gift of death could be seen as liberating and as loving as the gift of life.

Other Rituals

Letting go

There are various rituals for 'letting go'. At one of our sessions we each wrote all the things we wanted to let go of on a piece of paper and then tore them up and put them in a bowl of water. The intention was that the pieces of paper would sink and form compost for a water-lily - but they did not sink even when squeezed . . . and not even by the following morning. Millie asked, "Does this really do any good?" On reflection we thought that it at least affirmed intention and might be the first step in a thousand miles. Janet said that she liked the symbolism: the fact that the paper had not sunk was more realistic - the actual task of letting go was much more difficult and took time. On Sunday morning we squeezed out the paper and buried it! Would life could be as simple!

On one of our early weekends at Glastonbury we had access to the Abbey grounds and so were able to go in very early in the morning before all the tourists arrived. In a small chapel there we gathered in a circle with a bowl of water in the centre which we blessed. Then we took a large smooth stone and in silence each of us held it in turn for a few minutes as it was passed round the circle. As we held it, we focussed on all the hurt, grief and pain in our lives which we directed into the stone. When the stone had made a complete circle it was washed in the water. Glenys then carried the bowl outside and threw the water on to the grass. The stone was now passed round the circle again and this time we focussed on the blessings in our life and our love for each other. This was all in silence. Then we went outside to the Holy Thorn tree and laid the stone on its roots. Then we danced. Obviously such a ceremony did not take the pain away but it confirmed the empathy.

Another kind of ritual can release a long held grief. One woman related how she had never been able to express her grief for still-born twins; it was only many years later when an older woman enabled her to take part in a ceremony which she had convened with friends that she was able to express and release this long felt sadness.

Divorce

Betty James, who is a counsellor and one of our participants, devised a rite of passage for divorce. She wrote:

What we haven't got is a ceremony that would be relevant to an increasingly large proportion of the adult population - a ceremony for the ending of an intimate partnership. There is no way to acknowledge formally the regret, pain, sense of betrayal felt when promises once made, whether formally or informally, have to be cancelled. There is no way to formulate a 'clean break', psychologically as well as financially. In many separating couples the damaging resentment, hatred, sense of rejection and failure remain, often for a life-time, unsatisfactorily resolved.

There have been those whom I have counselled who longed to admit fault and failure before they moved on to other relationships or to changed lifestyles. They wanted a recognition before witnesses, or one witness, or just to each other that the failed marriage had been meaningful and the failure regretted before a fresh unencumbered start was made.

She devised a ceremony (when the divorce was based on mutual consent) with the two erstwhile partners and a witness whereby they recall the people they once were at the time they made their marriage vows, remembering the purity of that moment of sacred intent: 'a moment which can never be invalidated. It stands in time as a moment of truth and love, but through human frailty we sink from our high resolve'. The witness then asks each of them in turn if they accept responsibility for the failure of the marriage and ask forgiveness which the other partner gives. The witness then ends by saying:'In total forgiveness there is total healing, may you face the future in tranquillity and peace.'

Closure or saying farewell

Our exploration weekends last three days. By the time we have spent such time together, sharing our stories and exposing our vulnerability, we have generated a love and trust which needs an appropriate closure. So we have a ceremony to round off the weekend which is a way of blessing each person, thanking them and wishing them well for the future. It has evolved over the years and I hope is still evolving. In the early days we experimented with various ways of verbalising this, but it was unsatisfactory: some women liked to say too much, some found it an ordeal to say anything at all. Now we each in turn light a candle and hold it in front of us as we make eye contact with each person around the circle signifying our thanks, affirmation and blessing. This central ceremony is embroidered in a different way with each group. Usually there are some circle dances, some readings, sometimes a song and often what we call 'a Rosy Glow' (as opposed to 'a hot flush'!). A long strip of paper is provided for each woman (as for the game of 'Consequences'). Each writes her name at the bottom of the sheet and hands it to the person on her right. The next person writes a very simple affirming message at the top of the paper to the woman whose name appears at the bottom and then folds it over so that it cannot be seen. When all are ready it is passed on again. By the time this has been right round the circle, there is a small bundle which is then put in a pocket or handbag and not opened until the recipient gets home. It can provide a continuing warmth and blessing in the days ahead.

When women come for the second or third (or more) time we insert a ritual with milk and honey into our farewell ceremony. The little bowl of milk and honey is on the central table and when we come to the appropriate place one of the women picks it up and says:

With this milk symbolising the nurturing love of women
and honey, symbolising the energy of a co-operative community
We look forward, as the old prophecies foretold,

To a world flowing in milk and honey,
where children may live and love and grow in peace.
We now taste this in the hope that we may play our part in
bringing it about.

The bowl is then passed round and each of us dips her finger in and tastes. At the end of the ceremony we go out and walk to the centre of the labyrinth where the remains of the milk and honey are poured on the roots of the central tree of life. (Sometimes if we are running late or it is raining we will let this be done by a representative, at a later time.)

Labyrinth

The labyrinth itself is a spiritual tool and means different things to different people. To many it represents the twists and turns of the path through life. The labyrinth which is cut into the grass at the Grange is based on the pattern and dimensions of the one in Chartres Cathedral. It is a meditational path which is simply followed from the outside to the centre. (It is important to distinguish this from the maze which is a puzzle involving decisions as to which way to go.) When we first cut this into the grass my thought was that when people arrived for the beginning of a weekend we could all walk into the middle of the circle, dropping off our worries and problems from home on the way. Having arrived at the centre, we would walk directly back into the house. Then at the end of the retreat we could start the journey home by going to the centre and slowly walking out, picking up the threads of life at home (hopefully without the worries!) as we went. In the event it is usually not appropriate to do this on the first evening when everyone is tired (and it may be dark or raining), but we often use it at the end.

However, in its full glory there is more to it than this. In the centre of the circle there are six petals with a tree symbolising the Tree of Life. What are the significance of these petals? Lauren Artresse has written a book *Following the Sacred Path* in which she suggests a meditation at the centre. So when I reach there I follow her suggestion and stand for a few minutes in the first petal meditating on rocks and minerals (as being the building blocks of our planet), then move on to the second petal to meditate on vegetable life, animal life in the third and humanity in the fourth, 'angelic' life in the fifth and 'the unknown' in the sixth, thus bringing the process of evolution into consciousness and making us realise that far from being at the top of the tree, we are simply part of a process. It is exciting to realise that LIFE appeared apparently from nowhere between the first and second petals, LANGUAGE between the third and fourth. Maybe a higher form of LOVE is emerging between the fourth and fifth as we enter a new state of being which in this symbolism is termed 'the angelic'. Perhaps Teilhard might relate it to what he called 'the noosphere' - unconditional and all-embracing love.

Rhythms of the Day

Times of day mark the rhythm of our lives. At the Grange we start the day with half an hour shared silence which we preface with a prayer such as this Sanskrit one which we have adapted (changing the line which reads 'The glory of power' to 'The energy of love'):

> *Look to this day for it is life,*
> *The very life of life.*
> *In its brief course lie all*
> *The realities and truths of existence:*
> *The joy of growth,*
> *The splendour of action,*
> *The energy of love.*

For yesterday is but a memory
And tomorrow is only a vision,
But today well lived
Makes every yesterday a memory of happiness
And every tomorrow a vision of hope:
Look well therefore to this day.

or a Taoist meditation:

Close your eyes and you will see clearly.
Cease to listen and you will hear truth.
Be silent and your heart will sing.
Seek no contacts and you will find union.
Be still and you will move forward on the tide of the spirit.
Be gentle and you will need no strength.
Be patient and you will achieve all things.
Be humble and you will remain entire.

Outside of these weekends, however, many of us have our own routine for starting the day. My own routine goes like this:

I say a prayer for purification and wholeness in the shower and then, having made my husband and myself our morning cup of tea, I do some yoga practice. With deep breathing I connect to the different elements of earth, water, fire and air, then to the concept of growth and life, then to the 'Past, present and future in Now', then to the warmth, radiance and love of Christ from which base I send out blessings to different parts of the world.

On a fine summer morning it is a wonderful experience to stand on the grass barefoot in the garden and salute the sun with Suriya Namaskara (yoga) movements. Sadly there are few mornings in this country when I have done this but nevertheless it is also good to face in the direction of the sunrise and do it in the bedroom. I make it into a prayer for each of my family and friends and groups of people where I know there is a special need. It feels as though there is much more impetus behind a prayer which is said with the full strength of the body and breath, rather than just saying a name and wishing well. It gets the endorphins going and is also a good preparation for a twenty-minute session of meditation. This not only gives a good start to the day but for me provides a spiritual discipline to channel the energy of love.

One of the advantages of the second half of life is that it is possible to start the day off regularly with such a routine without the rush of the family getting off to school or office. Many of us have developed different routines once we have the space to do this. Like the Chinese, some start the day with Tai Chi and these people usually do manage to find somewhere to go outside. Some begin with prayer and reading. Others have a run during which they connect with nature.

Meals

I feel continuously grateful for everything so feel no need to make a special issue over food. I do not say grace because this seems to go back to the time when we were in the survival stage (as many people still are in our world today) and food was about the only thing we had to be thankful for.

But when we eat together as a group it is affirming to have a moment of silence before a meal and hold hands in gratitude and friendship. The ancient Christian 'love feast', using such words as 'the Bread of Life' and 'the Wine of Love' can embrace all taking part in the experience of family - 'That all may be one'.

It can also make a meal special if we look to see where our food came from and send out blessings and thanks to the countries from which the various components originated, whether from the garden, the local farm or from the other side of the world, and to give thanks to the people who prepared it. A simple meal can take us to many different countries. Some groups who have come to the Grange have eaten one meal in silence in order to appreciate the taste and texture of the food which again is another way of extending our awareness.

Several groups of Russian women have been to the Grange and they always greet us at the first meal in the same beautiful way. One of them represents them all. Over her outstretched hands lies a red and white embroidered cloth on which has been placed a round loaf and dish of salt. We are all invited to take a piece of bread and dip it into the salt before eating it. This affirms our eternal friendship.

End of the day
We usually end our days of exploration with a short silence and music. This is often the Celtic blessing:

> *Deep peace of the running wave to you,*
> *Deep peace of the flowing air to you,*
> *Deep peace of the silent stars to you,*
> *Deep peace of the quiet earth to you,*
> *May peace fill your soul,*
> *May peace make you whole.*

It is especially important for children to have a spiritual end to the day. This may involve lullabies, stories and perhaps bedtime prayers but most importantly some kind of thanksgiving and the knowledge that they are loved and valued.

Inner Strength

We often ask, 'From where do you draw inner strength or spiritual nourishment?' The answers include 'nature', 'the mountains', 'the sea', 'family','people' (those with whom we have a close relationship or perhaps someone who has found an inner strength of their own), 'worship within a like-minded community', 'music', 'poetry', 'beautiful buildings', 'a physical discipline' (such as yoga or Tai Chi,) 'silence', 'solitude', 'hearing the life story of others'.

For much of the time, gratitude is not only a natural response but is also life-giving. It can enhance our abundance of life if we create a 'string of pearls' as advocated by Marion Milner in her book (published at the age of eighty-seven) *Eternity's Sunrise - A way of keeping a diary*. Each day she would mark a good event which had occurred to her the day before, by a symbolic object until she had a string of these good memories like a 'string of pearls'. When Ann tried this she discovered that amid all the busy hustle of office and family life it was something like a telephone call and a moment of deeper human contact which was the most significant and life-enhancing moment giving her her 'pearl' for the day.

God

It may seem strange that in a chapter on spirituality I have not mentioned 'God'. Of course if I were a Buddhist this would be quite natural. Many of us have our own understanding of God and I respect others' belief and experience. For myself I have always had a yearning for something much greater than myself which I associate with unconditional love and which, as a child, I identified as God. Now I wonder whether this is an awareness of some future way of being.

Love

However, central to spirituality is love. All spiritual leaders tell us to love one another. So this is the subject of the next chapter.

And Then . . . ?

All these things can fruitfully be considered and developed in circle. It may be that some circles may then develop into a Spiritual Resource Circle as we envisaged in our afternoon sessions at St James' and which I record in the second half of 'My Story'.

These could form a nucleus in the community and would be available for healing, emotional, practical and spiritual support. They could also in themselves be sources of growth. Women's liturgical groups have often been formed for the purpose of a particular occasion such as 'One World Sunday' or 'Women's World Day of Prayer', but then disbanded. Perhaps they might be sustained with wider relevance in a multi-purpose Resource Group.

THEMES FOR CIRCLE CONSIDERATION

1. How do you find inner strength / spiritual nourishment?

2. Has there been any life-changing experience in your life?

3. Do you practise meditation? If so can you describe how and why you started and how the experience has been for you?

4. How do you find physical activity affects your sense of well being?

5. Where and when do you find time for solitude?

6. Can you suggest a symbol which has a powerful meaning for you?

7. Is there any place which feels especially sacred for you?

8. If you were writing Stephanie Sorrell's poem beginning 'If one day you find me gone . . . ' how would you continue?

7

LOVE

Love is the river of life in this world.
Think not that you know it who stand at the little tinkling rill,
the first small fountain.
Not until you have gone through the rocky gorges,
and not lost the stream;
Not until you have gone through the meadow,
and the stream has widened and deepened until
fleets could ride on its bosom;
Not until, beyond the meadow you have come to
the unfathomable ocean,
and poured your treasure into its depths,
Not until then can you know what love is.

Henry Ward Beecher

Slight shifts in imagination have more impact on living
than major efforts at change.

Thomas Moore

One day when we have mastered the winds, the tides
and gravity, we shall harness for God the energies of Love . . .
and then for the second time in the history of the world,
we shall have discovered fire.

Teilhard de Chardin

This is the chapter to which I hope you will give the most consideration. I have left it until near the end because it is only
when a circle has developed love and trust, when the members
of the circle feel able to listen sensitively and speak from the
heart on a deep level, that we can approach the truth of love.

The concept of 'love' seems first to have appeared in history about two thousand years BC when Confucius spoke of 'reng'. This however meant little more then 'Do as you would be done by' or 'Do not do unto others as you would not have done unto you'. He spoke of yielding to another person so that the self became diminished in the service of another. He realised that love could not be brought about by an act of will and he turned to music and ritual to try to create it.

Buddha also spoke of love and he considered the motivation behind acts of kindness or generosity.

The history of the Jews tells us that the first of their ten commandments was 'Thou shalt love the Lord thy God', but how does such love relate to love between human beings? Is such 'love' not more akin to 'worship'?

Christ's first commandment was to 'Love God' and the second was to 'Love your neighbour as yourself', and he went further in saying, 'Love one another as I have loved you', recognising that love is not something which can be taught in words but can only be shown by example. (Does it also imply that I am unable to love until I have been loved?)

About fourteen hundred years later St Francis enlarged the framework (and our concept of love) by saying, 'Make me an instrument of your peace (love)'. Now human beings were co-creators with God and our horizons had expanded again.

Love must surely be the key to future growth but there has been little development in our understanding of love since then. The basic assumption of popular psychology that our main driving force, at one level or another, is self-gratification does not help. It must surely be of immense significance that the word 'love' is so widely prevalent in literature, song and poetry, and just taken for granted, yet in psychology books love is rarely mentioned except in terms of what C. S. Lewis calls 'need love'.

We don't even have an adequate vocabulary to help us understand this word which covers a multitude of different meanings.

T. S. Eliot says: in 'East Coker:

. . . And so each venture
Is a new beginning, a raid on the inarticulate,
With shabby equipment always deteriorating
In the general mess of imprecision of feeling,
Undisciplined squads of emotion.

But need it remain like this?

Today many prefer to use the word 'altruism' but this does not seem to be adequate, suggesting an act of will. Our understanding of the word 'love' needs to be refined into a much more comprehensive interpretation of its reality and its potential. It is energising, creative, unifying.

We speak of 'conditional love' in relation to Jehovah of the Old testament who will love us (or perhaps just look after us) if we are good. On the other hand the 'unconditional love' of a person such as Christ promises love whatever we say or do.

If our lives are starved of love we are more possessive and defensive. Possessiveness causes a great deal of pain and limitation. The possessive assumption behind such songs as 'One alone to be my own' seems to set a pattern of fulfilment for those who find a partner, and a life of emptiness for those who do not. But lives filled with love are more capable of sharing and releasing others into freedom. Our love can be expressed in sexuality, in words and beyond words - in music, art, dance, action and silence. If we understood our emotions better couldn't this free up a greater potential for love? This is happening already but there is much more to understand.

In one of the places where we lived abroad, St Valentine's day coincided with a local festival in which pilgrims, clothed in white, came from all over the island in family groups to a central pool where they bathed in the waters as a rite of purification. As it was explained to me, this was a purifying ceremony to cleanse love - which I interpreted as a cleansing from lust and possessiveness and was in stark contrast to the possessive and often erotic cards being sent to each other by the British community. In retrospect I may have misunderstood the explanation given to me on that day of the local ceremony but what a wonderful idea it would be to have such a rite for the purification of love!

Another aspect worth considering is the way that the phrase 'greater love hath no man than this that a man lay down his life for his friend' has entered the very texture of our language and rightly reverberates on Days of Remembrance for the war dead. However, the assumption that the highest love can be demonstrated by dying is not something which we want to encourage today. (It could be echoed by suicide bombers and suicidal youngsters who feel they have no part to play in the community and are simply a burden to everyone else.) The greatest love can be shown by living life to the full, and by creating a world in which children can live and love and grow in peace - which may include working for peace and justice, creating songs or drama, and inspiring and nourishing others into a fuller life.

Varieties of Love

There are so many different varieties of love - probably as many as there are human beings on the earth.

Love is a word like 'colour' in that it covers a wide spectrum of possibilities. Whereas with colour we have words for primary - red, blue and yellow - and then an enormous variety of descriptions for the various hues and shades which enable us to say what we mean, we have no such counterpart in love. This one word, 'love', covers the extremes of sexual erotic obsession, sacrificial life-giving for a friend, and a woolly dutiful well-wishing.

In order to understand the dynamics of our emotions and increase our capacity for love don't we need to define at least some of these different meanings? Such definitions can mix and mingle like the waves of the sea but as we increase our awareness of such differences, we learn to articulate and handle the dynamics of love more maturely. We can at least make a beginning.

Love was supremely important to the Greeks and in the Pythagorean and Platonic systems. They saw God, or 'The One', as the very source of love. They recognised its different forms and functions, taking four meanings and functions as their starting point.

So perhaps we could take these as our 'primary colours' and then differentiate within these categories. I suspect that many women would not start from here but would approach it more as we did in our 'Friends of Sophia' circle (which I shall recount later) but as these definitions are embedded in the Western psyche I will make a start with them. The four meanings were: Philia, Storge, Eros and Agape.

Philia

Basically this means 'I like' or 'I enjoy', as in 'I love classical music, strawberries, playing the piano, climbing a mountain, Cliff Richard, Lesley Garrett'. It is a fact about me. There is no personal relationship involved although relationship is an essential part of the meaning of nearly all other meanings of the word 'love'.

Loving myself
This is a concept very widely used in modern psychology. Basically it means I like myself, I appreciate my own abilities and potential, I nurture myself and look after my needs and dreams. Again there is no relationship involved except between two aspects of the self. It seems to be a helpful concept for some people (especially if they come from a starting point of 'I hate myself') but can have no such creative affirmation as love given by another person or group of people.

My understanding of love is as a moving energy between two or more people so for me it makes no sense at all to speak of 'loving myself' (although I may rejoice and be grateful for who I am). Such a concept of self love seems to arise from a psychology which is based on the human being in isolation instead of looking at the dynamics of energy and magnetism flowing between . . . Did Descartes shut us into this box with his isolating first principle of 'I think therefore I am'? Could we not rather say, 'I love you, therefore you are'?

Storge

This is love of the type found in a family relationship: parental love, brotherly love, sisterly love and so on. Apart from the beginning of marriage, it is a *de facto* relationship. The family can be a container for both unconditional and conditional love or even just dutiful love. At least there is usually an assumption that, at some level, love or bonding exists. The word also means 'putting up with', which is an amusing comment on the way some family relationships have not changed much over the years. Some might want to describe it in terms of C. S. Lewis's 'need love'. In fact there has been quite a lot of research into such relationships in the field of family therapy so this is not such an uncharted area as other meanings of the word 'love'.

Marriage
In the past (and at the present time in some cultures), marriages were arranged and love was not always present but usually developed through the immediacy of contact and through deliberate fostering. The arrangement was often made on the basis of commercial transaction or political expediency which was clearly not a hopeful beginning. Today, in India, marriages are often arranged (not forced) by parents who aim to find compatible partners within a culture of shared values. Some of the happiest marriages have grown this way through deliberate generation of love and empathy for each other.

Throughout history it has been a basic assumption that

children are reared in the love and protection of a man and a woman. Beyond this there is the African saying that 'it takes a village to raise a child'. There is nothing more important for a child and growing adult than to know that he or she is loved. Such unconditional love is rarely found as yet outside the family (and too often is not sufficiently cultivated even there). Sue Gerhardt (in her book *Why Love Matters*) claims that affection actually shapes a baby's brain.

In the 'love match' of our recent Western culture, attraction is ideally on all three levels of body, mind and spirit. Very often it is simply 'eros'. The initial passion usually dies after some time and then (at least when children are involved) needs to be consciously converted into the stability of 'Storge'. More about this later.

Eros

This is the physically sexual love which saturates our present culture. There are clearly many subdivisions of this: heterosexual, homosexual, requited, unrequited, etc. Church fathers tried to reach for a higher experience of spiritual life by spurning pleasures of the flesh and demonising sexuality. In the process they condemned woman as a harlot while they worshipped Mary the mother of God who they believed had no experience of sex. For hundreds of years in our Western civilisation we almost lost the knowledge known by the ancient Sumerians, that sexuality can be sacred and beautiful. The realisation that it can be so, has largely coincided with the discovery of contraception and women's liberation so that the pendulum has now swung in the opposite direction and we have created a society obsessed with sex but with the sacred aspect now lost in casualness and exploitation. It is too often simply the satisfying of an appetite rather than the expression of love.

Can we rediscover the sacredness of sex - the deepest expression of love between two people as well as the initiation of new life? This may be difficult so long as some religious leaders assume that in order to dedicate their lives to God they need to reject sexuality as something sinful and are shocked by the suggestion that Jesus might have been in love with Mary Magdalene. Such men need to overcome their fear of women and discover an 'equal but different' relationship between men and women which can lead us into a more balanced future.

Courtly love

This was not experienced or described by the Greeks but this seems an appropriate place to consider it. This is a very interesting phenomenon usually associated with 'The Age of Chivalry' in Western Europe. It has been suggested that a love which began with Eros was deliberately sublimated on to a spiritual level. If this was so, it suggests a spiritual technique which is little known today. On the other hand it is probable that the knight was initially magnetised by a spiritual quality within the lady whom he loved, rather than by physical attraction. Either way, such a chaste relationship between a knight and his lady was the subject of many troubadours' songs as they serenaded romantic love and was clearly a source of inspiration for him, if not for her.

Such themes are also echoed in poetry by Shakespeare and other poets: such was the love of Dante for Beatrice, and other poets speak of their 'Muse', who may have no idea of the role she is playing. In fact such a 'romantic' love may be more prevalent even today than we realise. The ecstasy of unrequited love can be very real even if (and perhaps especially *if*) the object of such passion knows nothing about it. Few would admit to this but it surely happens. What does it mean? Is there a significance here which we are missing?

Agape

For Christians this word means a Christlike love in which all are invited to share.

When I was first introduced to the idea, it was described in terms of a conscious effort of will. I could understand a duty to help someone and ensure their well-being but it seemed so cold, bland and lacking in empathy. This was not how I understood the word 'love'.

Very often in the past (and perhaps today) charity workers were motivated in their 'good works' by the hope of earning Brownie points in Heaven. Where is the love in that situation? No wonder we have used the phrase 'cold as charity'.

However, I know from my experience in the church to which I now belong that when a group of people respond to a need in the wider community and manifest their care - for the homeless, the ex-prisoner, the lone parent or others - by giving support, this develops into love. What is not remarked on, however, is the love which has grown among those who have worked together to bring this about. This is how I now understand 'Agape'.

Such love can emerge in circle, too, after sharing stories which reveal vulnerability and evoke empathy and support. This is not a focussed love by one person for another but in this situation rather a way of being.

I refer later to 'inspirational love' which has the same characteristic of focussing on some area beyond the two or more people who are involved rather than on each other.

Transcendent love

This is the kind of love which we recognise in such people as Jesus Christ, the Buddha, the Dalai Llama, Mother Theresa, etc. It is a love for all, outflowing from the heart centre and is unconditional. It is characteristic of someone who has transcended into a new way of being. Some of us may also have known this experience for brief periods. Such people can themselves be a source of Agape.

Friendship

This can be a life-giving relationship and covers an infinite variety of degrees of intensity. It can be based on shared experiences, memories and mutual interests. Primarily it is affirming and supportive. There is usually a reciprocity of giving and receiving in whatever form. On the whole this is a low-energy-level relationship. However, it may develop into a high energy state through the libido and become Eros, or through the intellect and become platonic, or through the spirit and become inspirational love. Isn't it true that all human beings flourish on friendship? We are not creatures of isolation.

Sophia Explorations into Love

'Sophia' means female wisdom and I described in the second half of 'My Story' how our 'Friends of Sophia' came into being. In such a circle we all know each other and it is easier to create a pool of love and trust deep enough to consider 'love'. In the summer of 2005 we had a weekend devoted to this theme.

Instead of taking as our starting point the different varieties of love analysed by the philosophers as above, we started from a consideration of how love was for us in different relationships. Those of us fortunate enough to have been nourished by love in our childhood, affirmed that we have a natural outreach towards our fellow human beings.

We started by meditating on some of the main aspects of love in our experience and then describing how we felt.

We began with our response to *a child - a young baby*. This is probably the easiest person to love because of the vulnerability and innocence. Our love is tender and protective.

Secondly, we considered the kind of love we felt towards *a mother*. The intention was that we should imagine the ideal, archetypal mother for whom we would feel warmth and security . . . However, for several people this was overlaid by feelings for the real mother they had known which were sometimes far from this. In such cases it is interesting how in some cases Mary (the mother of Jesus) has been adopted as a substitute, and may partly explain the veneration in which she has been held down the centuries - almost as a female deity.

Thirdly, we considered our feelings towards *someone who was suffering*. There was compassion - but this situation also called forth feelings of helplessness, anger, sometimes guilt and the feeling that one ought to be sympathetic but needed to be detached in order to give support. In this situation, rather than being involved or detached, there is a third way of the yogi who comes from the point of inner stillness and can both empathise totally, yet because of inner strength can provide support. This is something which needs to be cultivated by a yoga discipline over the years and cannot be an instant reaction.

Fourthly, we considered our feelings for *an inspiring teacher*. Of course there may be physical attraction or the natural magnetism of someone who cares about the welfare of the student, as a good teacher usually will, but beyond that there is the teacher-pupil relationship *per se*, which is so often misunderstood at the present moment and which can be a source of true richness, and growth. The distinction was made between the teacher who sees the potential of some student and enables this to emerge and the teacher who, by introducing a whole new body of knowledge to the pupil, opens the door to a new world. In either case this may result in a meeting of minds and an intense loving relationship, which would be identified as 'falling in love' particularly on the part of the pupil. I would want to call this 'inspirational love' which has nothing to do with physical attraction but is often interpreted in these terms and crushed. It can be a significant event in the life of the pupil (and sometimes the teacher too) but the teacher must know how to handle it and allow the pupil to acknowledge the love they feel as a source of growth and enrichment of life and then move on. Such a relationship has been recognised in some cultures as part of the growing up process, but has no recognition in our society.

Fifthly, we considered '*Falling in love*' in its wider sense. This is a vital phenomenon for which I have found no adequate psychological explanation. It does not help that some people (including academics) have never known this experience. We do not understand what it is, nor why it happens (other than to assume that it is entirely about mating), so we laugh about it and dismiss it as a 'kind of madness which does not last very long'.

Not so. It may be ephemeral or it may last a life-time. In this state we probably feel more fully alive than at any other time. In a psychology based on the self it is theorised that all we are doing is falling in love with a projection of our own *animus*. Yet, some of us know that it is an experience of encounter with another, however idealised our perception of that person may be. In my experience it is essentially the attraction of something beyond my present limits - 'The desire of the moth for the star' (or the candle flame which will burn it to death)! Perhaps we are seeing some potential which needs to be affirmed?

There is no way we can will ourselves to 'fall in love' - nor to escape from it. It is not just a manifestation of hunger - or need - as it can happen to those whose lives are surrounded by love. So what is the significance of this? Why does the world seem to be in harmony and life so joyous when we are 'in love' (however inappropriate may be the object of our affection) and why are we tipped into misery and despair when we are deprived of such a love? It can also occasionally escalate into a dangerous obsession, especially when entangled with possessiveness and such situations will attract psychological attention. However, because we do not understand *why* it happens, we often do not reveal it when it happens, or we dismiss it with a giggle. Erich Fromm from his classical book *The Art of Loving* dismisses the phenomenon of 'falling in love' as of little account.

In our circle we felt that, whatever the experience was, it enabled a part of ourselves to grow, but it need not have anything to do with future marriage or partnership. We again talked about the love based on an affinity of thought or a common vision. This could be the love between a pupil and teacher as already considered, or the inspirational love between two people with a common vision, which also has no recognition in our society (this may be more common in later life). Perhaps, instead of dismissing it as 'madness' we should consider whether 'falling in love' could be a clue to a future evolving humanity in which we might have a greater capacity to love and for which the creative energy of inspirational love could be a key. I will return to this.

Finally we talked about *transpersonal / transcendental* love or the kind of mystical experience in which a person feels at one with the cosmos - loving all fellow human beings, outside time, ecstatically joyful and with increased awareness through the senses. This may happen in a 'peak experience' for a few moments or it may happen for longer periods, often changing lives and providing a new paradigm of the world. Some people said that they did not know this experience and we thought at the time that it could not be deliberately induced, although now it seems that an awareness of the possibility, combined with an open heart, an inner stillness and amid the wonder of nature it might come about. (See also chapter on Spirituality.) It has a resemblance to 'inspirational falling in love'.

There are so many other aspects of love to be explored. When we came to paint symbols representing our experience of love, one picture showed thorns and chains. This is a darker side of love which also needs exploration as do 'tough love', 'dutiful love', and a myriad more, but we aim to consider these in a dynamic experiential context, and there need to be many other similar research projects.

The Friends of Sophia have met every summer since 2005 to consider aspects of love.

I said at the beginning that identifying the various aspects of love is like trying to identify waves of the sea. They roll into each other, reform and break up only to flow in again from the wide ocean. As we begin to identify these various aspects (especially the largely unrecognised experiences of inspirational love) and to understand the dynamics of 'falling in love', so we shall be able to grow into a new way of life. It is something which we cannot do on our own. It needs the sharing of many, many more life stories and the kind of exploration which can be cultivated within our circles. Women are usually more prepared to explore their emotional life than men. As yet we may be no better at controlling our feelings, but if we learn to discriminate more skilfully between different experiences of love this may lead on to discovering further distinctions and eventually enable emotional maturity for both men and women to balance the intellectual levels which exist at the present time.

I shall now repeat what seems to me the most important feature of this chapter. The fact that inspirational love is often mistaken for Eros means that many potentially creative relationships are denied if they seem 'inappropriate'. Our society has been conditioned to believe that we can only really love one person and that this will automatically be manifested through physical sexuality. This often means that anything else which feels as powerful must be made taboo. Inspirational love, when unrecognised as such, can be quite scary because there is a feeling, conditioned by society, that it may be 'wrong' some-how. It may also be true that it is only those who have felt truly loved who are able to make this distinction, because where there is a hunger for love, *any* kind of love may be seized upon.

I will now examine Inspirational love in more detail.

Inspirational Love

I suggest that this is a love between two or more people who share the same vision or concern. It is far more intense than friendship and is bursting with potential in the spiritual or emotional field - yet there is probably no physical attraction or physically sexual component. Examples of this would be St Francis and St Clare, George Fox and Margaret Fell, Sri Aurobindo and 'The Mother', Teilhard de Chardin and Lucile Swan, and many more unidentified. The focus is not primarily on each other but on something beyond. There is joy and affirmation in the existence of such a relationship and in communication, but not necessarily in the physical presence of each other. I suspect that such a love could even emerge from a correspondence, perhaps by e-mail, with someone on the other side of the world.

Love is characterised by its creative energy. There is a physical attraction between male and female in both humans and animals which generates new life. Beyond this, the attraction of mind and spirit can likewise generate abundant growth and new understanding.

Because such love is not identified it is often denied. If the focus is on a shared vision or interest rather than on each other, it need pose no threat to existing relationships. This of course depends on any existing marriage being strong and deeply loving. It is also vital to ensure that inspirational love has been accurately identified; without this the new attraction could be damaging and hurtful.

While recognising that such relationships can slip across from one variety to another, with sufficient awareness this need not happen. Most of us already recognise that the quality of our lives depends on our relationships. If future generations could become more aware of the different nature of these then the quality of life - the level of joy, energy and creativity could be much higher than it is today. There are many examples of falling in love in our literature and poetry but almost always seen in the context of a second love threatening the first. Without possessiveness, this need not be so and may be one of the ways in which we increase our capacity for loving

Finally, I should like to speak from my own experience. I have been increasingly concentrating on this phenomenon of 'falling in love'. Although it is usually dismissed as of no consequence, for me it has always had a major impact on my life. It seems that some people never fall in love, so to them it is meaningless. Those who do have the experience often find that once it has faded, the intensity of the experience is completely forgotten.

For me it has been unmistakable. It makes me feel fully alive, with heightened perception and hugely energised. It may last for only a few weeks or years but could provide a basis for further, more mature relationship, or for immense creativity in other fields. In my life inspirational love was not connected with any mating intention.

I should perhaps explain at this point that I have never experienced physical sexuality except within marriage. This may have been partly due to the fact that there were no sure methods of contraception when I was young - also the tenets of a Methodist upbringing go deep! - but it was mainly because I felt I had a vocation which precluded marriage and because, in any case, there was so much going on in my life. In fact I was very glad of these constrictions as most of the interesting men I knew also respected the code and it was possible to talk about things which mattered more to me (eg, 'Do people and their ideas have more impact on the course of history than battles?' 'How to tackle world poverty' 'How do different sorts of music affect people?' 'Why do some people have gifts such as healing, clairvoyance and others not?') without the distraction and assumption of a sexual agenda. Yes, it can be said that I lived too much in my head rather than in my heart, but this did not prevent me falling in love.

Such phenomena are like strong uncharted and largely unacknowledged currents moving beneath the surface of our society. The very existence of a person who is loved in this special way may be a source of gratitude and inspiration for the person who is doing the loving even though the object of such love may know nothing about it.

As I recounted in my story, during the course of my life I have been in love a number of times and from the perspective of my eighties I begin to see some significance. Two of these experiences of falling in love I would describe as 'inspirational': my love for Jill, my teacher, and for the man I called Paul. In both cases such love co-existed with an already existing love. It was as if my capacity for loving had been expanded, rather as a mother's capacity for loving is increased as each new child arrives. In fact the blossoming of love for each of my four children when they were born was for me very like falling in love, in the sense that there is a spontaneous outpouring of loving energy on to a new person. However, the love for a new baby is quite different in its nature from the adult 'inspirational love' which involves a shared passion, or vision or goal on which attention is focussed, rather than primarily on the other person. For me there was a hunger for communication.

Nearly thirty years ago the truth of inspirational love first emerged for me, like a pearl seen in the muddy depths of the water. I tried to grasp it and convey it, but it was fragile and all I could do was to try to express it in fiction form in a book called 'The Estuary' as a basis for discussion and consideration, hoping that it would resonate with other lives (which in many cases it did). This was the book I have already mentioned.

I am certainly not advocating that we always 'follow our heart' when we fall in love. Life is far more complex than that and other people are also involved. It may be appropriate; it may not. But our growth into a new way of being probably involves increasing our capacity to love. Inspirational love could be the gateway to this.

It may help to write in more detail about my own experience although I find it quite difficult to write about this because it may be difficult for many people to understand. When I met Paul he was trying to bring a new immediacy and reality into the Church. I knew plenty of people who were simply abandoning their religion as having little meaning for their lives. I knew plenty more who were aware of the emptiness of much of the old traditions but who did not know what to do about it. But then I met this man who was actually trying to introduce some fresh understanding and more imaginative ways of thinking; yet he was limited by a mindset derived from a male culture of over-intellectualisation and little emotional awareness, which to me seemed part of the problem. He did not believe that women had any understanding of spirituality so was not convinced by my own search for the sacred in our daily lives. But to me it all seemed part of finding a spiritual reality. He saw a huge spiritual potential in Mauritius because of the opportunity to share insights and festivals between the different religions. Paul and I disagreed about many things but at least he understood (or seemed to understand) what I was talking about. It was he who lent me the books written by Teilhard de Chardin and with him I could share my first excitement at these new ideas. He did not share my sense of enlightenment and liberation because he was not convinced by the argument, but he was interested in the effect of these ideas on me.

But then I fell deeply in love with him. This was something which I never dreamed would happen and would have tried to avoid.

Of course the obvious question at this point is why did I not just keep quiet about it and sweep it under the carpet? Because of my 'Realisation' experience, it was vital to be totally transparent and allow the truth and strength of new experience to find its own way through. Which is what happened. The new love was strong, true and energising. It could not be contained and I knew must have some meaning. Yet unlike other experiences of 'falling in love', I felt no physical attraction, nor did I want any new special relationship. Paul was a loner and it was fortunate that he made it clear that he did not want any relationship either. In effect this cleared the way later for occasional communication, as the boundaries were set. So what was it all about then?

Of course I loved him for his passion for justice, his courage, compassion and his dedication - as anyone would - but the key to my new state of being was the discovery of someone who was pursuing the same kind of spiritual reality which I had been looking for all my life.

My love for Alec was now mature and strong and it was probably only because of this that I felt able to explore with him what was happening, and my love for him grew immensely in the process.

In all our experience, in poetry and literature, 'falling in love' threatens an existing relationship as if it is only possible to love one person. As I tried to understand, my first thoughts were that it could be an increase in my capacity to love in the same way as the love for a new child. In my book 'The Estuary' I envisaged a second love co-existing harmoniously and creatively with the first. I believe this could be possible. But this was not my own experience.

My second attempted explanation was in terms of Teilhard de Chardin. Since Paul had introduced me to his writings was I really in love with Teilhard? (There was some physical resemblance.) But no.

Thirdly, I realised that it was similar to my experience of falling in love with Jill, my teacher, so many years ago. This had been based on a common love for poetry and literature and had co-existed with an existing love. True, Paul was not my teacher but we had a shared interest with the intellectual and emotional excitement which this can evoke. This still seems the most likely explanation although 'inspirational love' was (and is) as yet an unidentified concept, so is not yet accepted in the world as it is today. This is something which we urgently need to explore. As a preliminary definition I would describe it as a situation where two or more people share a common vision or objective, with the focus on this rather than on each other.

I can define this today but thirty years ago I was still trying to make sense of it. At that time I realised that it had no place in my life and needed to be contained. But it was too powerful to be denied or annihilated.

However, I then found that Teilhard had given me the answer. 'One day, after we have mastered the winds, the tides and gravity, we shall harness for God the energies of love and then for the second time in the history of the world, we shall have discovered fire.' The key word here was 'harnessed'. Maybe in the same way as my Realisation experience had been sustained by spiritual practice, so now could my love be contained. I already practised a yoga routine every morning and evening followed by meditation (a practice dedicated to something beyond myself) and realised that an intensification of this in the context of my love could transform the energies into something sacred. My love now became simply a sacred and joyous component of my inner life for which I was grateful, but had no part in my outer life at that time. Later, it was to be the source of energy and inspiration for most of what I have described in the chapter on Spirituality and also led me to the concept of resource groups.

My love for Alec remained as strong as ever. Some readers may find this hard to understand as few have the experience of a dedicated, consistent, spiritual practice. I simply tell you what happened to me. Because of this, I have, up to now, tried to explain what happened purely in terms of 'inspirational love', which is true . . . but not the whole truth, as it perhaps gives the impression that Paul and I, having discovered a common vision, discussed our insights together. This was not the case. We hardly communicated. The theory of 'inspirational love' may explain why I fell in love with him, but not what happened next, and because it seemed so unlikely that anyone would believe me, I have not expanded on this before. All I can say is that this is what happened. I suspect that any similar spiritual practice such as Tai Chi could have the same possibilities. Paul inspired and energised my future spiritual quest, initially in hopes that I could discover for him some way of making his own experience real and meaningful. But we communicated only rarely during the remainder of our time on the island and only by my twice yearly letters after we returned home until he died in 1998. After this I felt deeply committed to a quest which seemed to have a much wider significance.

As a result of this experience I suggest we need to look at this experience of 'falling in love' in a far wider context.

We are unused to examining our emotions in this critical way and it is only after a life-time's consideration of these issues that I feel able to offer these suggestions. They need to be compared and tested against the experience of others. In the nest of a loving and trusting woman's circle, I have sometimes been able to relate my experience and find occasional resonance, and always sympathetic consideration. Unfortunately, within the limits of our present vocabulary, unless you have personal knowledge of this kind of experience yourself, such a perception seems incomprehensible. Everyone who has fallen in love thinks they know what this means and assumes that every experience is basically the same. It is not. I do not quote the experience of others. It is vital that we only speak from our own experience.

Is this experience of inspirational love an emerging new phenomenon during the last two millennia? It brings the head and the heart together. Is it a new energy which will create a new world?

Perhaps women's circles - Sophia Circles - will be able to bring this concept to maturity. If so we should be able to increase our capacity for loving, and streams of creative energy would pour forth into the world.

LOVE: THEMES FOR CONSIDERATION

1. Why do we often laugh when anyone talks about 'falling in love'?

2. What has been your experience of falling in love?

3. Why do some experiences of 'falling in love' seem to be so unexpected and devoid of any creative future?

4. Have you experienced 'inspirational love'? If so, how did you handle it - and how did others perceive it and react?

5. Is loyalty often confused with possessiveness?

6. How do we increase our capacity for love?

7. Could the energy of inspirational love lift humanity into a new way of being?

8. To what extent do you think inspirational love is associated with the experience of transcendence?

HOPE FOR THE FUTURE:
A SEA-CHANGE

*Humankind is being lead along an evolving course . . . and
though we appear to be sleeping, there is an inner wakefulness
that directs the dream . . . and that will eventually startle us
back to whom we are.*

Rumi

*The human heart can go the lengths of God.
Dark and cold we may be, but this
Is no winter now. The frozen misery
Of centuries breaks, cracks, begins to move;
The thunder is the thunder of the floes,
The thaw the flood, the upstart spring.
Thank God our time is now, when wrong
Comes up to face us till we take
The longest stride of soul men ever took.
Affairs are now soul size,
The enterprise
Is exploration into God.
Where are you making for? It takes
So many thousand years to wake
But will you wake for pity's sake?*

From 'Sleep of prisoners' by Christopher Fry

*And all shall be well
And all manner of things shall be well
When the tongues of flame are in-folded
Into the crowned knot of fire
And the fire and the rose are one.*

from 'Little Gidding' by T. S. Eliot quoting Julian of Norwich

Nearly twenty years ago Mikhail Gorbachev and Ervin Laszlo, with others, called a World Forum to consider the future. Invitees were leaders in the fields of science, politics, economics and spirituality. Such a Forum has taken place every year since then. In 2005 it took place in Tokyo with the theme 'Creating a New Civilisation' and was attended by 4,000 people from forty-six different countries. Dr Ervin Laszlo stated that the next evolution of humanity will depend on a new convergence between science and spirituality. In the Tokyo Declaration drawn up at this conference Laszlo explains that 'the diverse crises we now face are, at core, a crisis of consciousness'. The Declaration asks us to 'facilitate and accelerate the blossoming of a higher form of civilisation that will embody the global wisdom of humankind, in order the entire human family may flourish with all of nature in this precious planet.' In the past few years it has emerged that we need to take decisive action within the next four years if we are to save the planet from global warming. Laszlo remains optimistic: 'In creating a new planetary civilisation, we must first fire up a critical mass of organised global citizens.'

A change in human consciousness will not come about by one enormous organised event but rather by the multiplicity of small groups - Wisdom Circles?

Never before have we had so many people with over half a life-time's experience on which to base their wisdom. Never before has there been such potential.

It is no good just sighing and wishing that things were different. Armageddon may be expected by some to descend on us from the outside. However, each one of us is the very fabric of potential change and it is by our words, actions, thoughts and prayers that a shift in consciousness could come. Could the essence of this be an increase in our capacity to love?

We may encounter ridicule from those who try to crush our vision of the future into old thought patterns but the least we can do is to have the courage to take the plunge and explore.

We all have ideas of how the future could be and now is the opportunity to share these. Let me make a start by sharing my vision.

My Vision - A Possible Scenario?

Our world is moving on, and the speed of change is increasing year by year. But the direction we are moving in is mainly determined by history. The intellectual development of a world which has been largely framed by men has gathered speed and momentum at the expense of our emotional maturity. We now need to change direction so that we can find a balance.

Stephen Hawking in his study of the universe comes to the conclusion that the driving principle behind it all is entropy. He sees the whole cosmos declining gradually into oblivion. However, as an astronomer he has left a vital component out of his equation - the factor of Life. Life regenerates, heals, reproduces in abundance and it is in this awareness that we need to live. Maybe the doom-laden future foretold for our planet could be countered by the creative genius of humanity.

Many Christians across the world today are obsessed with concepts of Armageddon rather than focussing on Christ's promise: 'I came that ye might have life and have it more abundantly'.

We are constantly surrounded by threats of global warming leading to the destruction of the planet yet maybe the co-operation of those who experience a new way of being could find a solution to these problems. For many years there has been talk of a 'shift of consciousness' and this is happening already. (The World Forum has spawned a website 'World Shift Network'.) Groups of people are getting together because something needs to be done without expecting the government or someone else to take the responsibility. The *Big Issue* defines it as a shift from the 'Me Society' to the 'We Society'. It involves sharing our resources and working out new ways of operating.

We have been living in an atmosphere of impending doom for most of our recorded history. But now we have the opportunity to move into a climate of hope.

Teilhard de Chardin (who was both a scientist and a priest) prophesied that humanity was on the verge of an evolutionary leap as great as that of the leap into language (and he associated this with women). He referred to this new way of being as the 'linking of minds' and perhaps in this he foresaw the internet. However, a leap suggests a radically new approach. He was not specific about this.

Could the leap be from intellectual to emotional development? From a goal of increasing consumption to a quest for spiritual and emotional growth? From an emotional level mainly based on what C. S. Lewis calls 'need love' to the overflowing of loving energy? From competition to co-operation? From left brain to right brain development? From a focus on the individual to an awareness of the energies flowing between us? From dualism to holism? From religion to spirituality? From the certainties and conflicts of the Tree of Knowledge to the love and creativity of the Tree of Life?

If we try to imagine what it must have been like for the apes who were first emerging into an awareness of speech, it would have been a tenuous exploration of a vast unknown. We can envisage that they would have had sudden sparks of communication when they began to have a dim awareness of what was happening. Perhaps one or two of them might get the hang of things quicker than the rest, although it would not be something which a single ape could discover on his own. (Maybe he fell in love with a woman and wanted to tell her - or possibly, since women seem to be prime communicators, it was the other way round!) They could have had no conception of the world into which they were moving - poetry, mathematics, physics would have been completely beyond their comprehension; a symphony orchestra would have seemed hilarious. And yet . . . and yet . . . it happened and occasionally there must have been a person here or there who emerged from this quagmire of puzzlement into a clearer light.

Maybe we are in the same situation today? We need to open our minds to unknown possibilities rather than seizing on instant solutions. There seems to be an innate longing for unity throughout all peoples of the world 'that we all may be one'. Such a search becomes ecstasy in transcendent moments when we experience a kind of unity with the whole cosmos. This is surely a clue. And love itself must be a clue.

In the early stages of evolution single small units joined together to make a more complex one. Could something similar be happening today? The magnetism which drew these early particles together could be analogous to the 'falling in love' experiences which we have today - often quite inappropriate, often only temporary, but finding a tendril magnetised towards another person usually in the hope of reciprocation, which makes us feel that this is the way life could be - an ecstasy of connection, and happening not only on the physical level, but on the intellectual and the spiritual level as well.

At the same time there is enormous suffering when a strong thread is broken. And in the world as we know it today, suffering seems inevitable, if only due to natural disaster, mistakes or human frailty. Can we find any significance in this?

It has always been a fundamental problem of Christianity that a loving God could allow his children to suffer. There have been theories of punishment and of testing, all set in the context of the past. Let us set this way of thinking aside and look at it in the context of the future. What actually happens at a time of suffering?

Often a whole community is drawn together in grief and we all become more aware of deeper levels of being. Could not this suggest that the seeds of more complex development are latent in the human condition? This is not to say that there is any 'virtue' in suffering or that it 'serves a purpose' but simply that it is part of evolving life. Such a philosophy brings little balm to the pain but it could help us to accept what is happening and to affirm it.

There could be many *clues which are pointing us towards a new state of being.*

1. *The emergence of groups.* In the past there have been huge movements of humanity supporting ideological or religious or patriotic aims. There has been community support based on locality or family, or a common trade. These still exist. But in addition, during the last fifty years or so there has been a proliferation of smaller groups: support groups, prayer groups, meditation groups, action groups, reading groups, common interest groups with the consequent creation of new relationships. Above all, groups of people getting together to do something which needs to be done rather than waiting to be paid or waiting for the government to do it.[22]

As I write, a flock of small birds is wheeling fast through the winter sky to settle together briefly on the branches of a bare tree and then, after a moment, take off again and circle around, landing on the telephone wires which stretch across the valley. They move as with one mind in perfect harmony and synchronicity. This is a phenomenon which we do not understand and yet which may have great significance for the future of humanity.

2. Is it not possible that through the ages *some people (Buddha? Jesus? St Francis? the Dalai Lama?) have already crossed this evolutionary threshold into a new way of being?* They have been intuitively recognised as 'special'. They have not been isolated figures but have created a group of men and women around them bound by love.

In the time of Christ, people's minds were formed in the pattern of Judaic religion. When they encountered Jesus, and recognised that here was someone special, how could they describe him, except in terms of 'The Son of God'? In the Far East, Buddha was described in terms of 'Enlightenment'. The Dalai Lama was special from birth and we can call him just the Dalai Lama! Many saints and unrecognised people through the centuries may have crossed this threshold. We may have called some of them 'Saints' and failed to recognise others.

3. A third clue may lie in the way *technology is developing in enabling us to have more communication* and more awareness through television, mobile phones, the internet.

4. Fourthly, perhaps we need to look at possible *latent faculties within ourselves* such as telepathy, clairvoyance, healing powers. Some people have been able to develop them. Many of us know that telepathy happens between two people who are in love.

5. *The mystical /transpersonal experience* which I have described in the book is now no longer confined to a few people but is becoming a much more common experience and must surely have significance for any future evolution. In fact, it may be that everyone has such experiences but does not always pause to consider what this could mean.

Yet these are only clues and we need to be able to live with an acceptance of the immensity of our 'unknowing'.

For thousands of years mankind had a struggle to survive and the objectives were therefore to accumulate as much as possible in the way of food, clothing and shelter. Now, for many, at least in the Western world, we have moved beyond the survival level into the opportunity for growth and development Yet old habits still prevail of accumulating material possessions in the belief that this is what life is all about. If those above the survival level turned their attention to the possibilities of growth and emotional maturity this could create a new generosity of spirit and clarity of mind which would release enormous resources into the developing world where survival is still a major concern. It would also open up new vistas of experience as yet unknown.

Survival of the fittest may have been the criteria for evolution in a world struggling for survival, but as we move into areas of spiritual growth, this criteria is changing. Already we look after and value our disabled and those with special needs and recognise that they too have a contribution to make (and maybe in the process our own capacity for compassion grows). Further evolution is no longer a matter of physical fitness but rather of conscious choice.

It may be tempting to leave all this to the geneticists now that claims are being made about selecting genes for personality formation, but even if this became possible it could never replace the cultural development of human beings into people with fully developed potential and the further development of creative communities.

The climate of our assumptions, attitudes, dreams, emotional intelligence and awareness could be building up to a critical point when there would be a shift. Love would become more widespread, life more abundant and vast creative energy would be released. There would be a shift away from the expectation of doom to a hope for a whole new way of being. There would be a sea-change.

Every single one of us, man and woman, old and young is part of this process. However, for various reasons, women are usually more in touch with their emotional life than men and more prepared to explore it. It is more frequently they who have hands-on experience of birth and death, care for the suffering and nurture the growing child. Many men are involved in this aspect of life, but they are not yet among the majority. As women are becoming increasingly confident and articulate, they are more able to explore their emotional lives and find healing. Women with half a life-time's experience behind them are in an especially favourable position. Some may be counsellors, healers or therapists; some may be working with mediation and conflict resolution; some belong to support groups, to action groups or prayer/meditation groups. Sometimes if they have been able to find a degree of wholeness and emotional maturity themselves, their very being may bring a healing element into a situation. Simply listening with full attention and without judgement can affirm a creative path into the future. It could be a step on the way to allowing humanity to grow into a whole new way of being.

When I first encountered the ideas of Teilhard de Chardin, his ideas were new and mostly rejected. However, they are now almost mainstream as so many groups have started exploring what such ideas could mean and looking towards a brilliant and hopeful future.

My conviction is that the circles of women now proliferating around the world could become circles of men and women bringing us to a wisdom where amazing things could happen.

Should we awaken to the truth of the moment, we can consciously usher in one of the most important human breakthroughs in history. We have the opportunity to forge a marriage between masculine and feminine, more potent and more vibrant than any we have experienced on the earth for ages - more beautiful perhaps, than any the earth has ever known.

Marianne Williamson

It's up to us - to me and you.

APPENDIX 1

In June, July, August 1985, we had some afternoon sessions at St James', Piccadilly, to explore the possibility of Resource Groups for women. Danielle Arin (Lessware) was unable to come to our session on Body-Mind Integration, but sent us this contribution instead.

YOGA - AN INSPIRATION

Yoga came to me when I lost a child - it came through a perceptive friend, although at the time the word 'yoga' had not been mentioned to me. The tragedy I was living filled my whole being with rebellion, bitterness and scepticism. In time, yoga turned these feelings into acceptance, understanding and above all the discovery of signs of spiritual awareness within myself and later on, within others.

After five years of steady practice, I was asked to teach. I felt I had by then enough self-knowledge and dedication to have the courage to answer the call. I accepted the challenge, believing that this was the best way I could serve. In gratitude for what yoga did for me and my development in life, I wanted to impart my knowledge and conviction to others . . . within my limitations of course, but always trying to reach further and better.

Of the many aspects of yoga which fascinates me, the correlation between the eight limbs of yoga (as described in the second chapter of Patanjali's *Yoga Sutra*) and the attitude to the postures always strikes me as being the most significant. For through this, yoga becomes an integral discipline of postures, behaviour, breathing, concentration, meditation and joy.

Yoga is not a religion, nor does it claim to be a substitute for religion. But although it requires no adherence to a dogma, it does urge the observance of the dual ethic of yama and niyama. A sentence which has always affected the way I practise yoga is B.K.S. Iyengar's opening to Part Two of *Light on Yoga*: 'Practice of asanas without the backing of yama and niyama is mere acrobatics.'

Yama
(or social moralities)

Yama has five principles, each of which can be applied to teaching and practising:

1. Non-violence/love (**ahimsa**) requires a careful and sensitive approach to the postures which should nevertheless be firm and challenging; in harmony in the performance of a pose in order to show respect for the body; purification of the mind and body from their limitations and ailments so as to render them a better temple for the soul.

2. *Truth* (**satya**) augments the quality of a pose by right thinking and performance to avoid any possibility of inner challenge and confusion. When working with truth, fruit of actions come without apparently doing anything.

3. *Non-stealing* (**asteya**) can be interpreted to mean that teachings should be absorbed, digested and understood, then forgotten and relearned through one's own practice. By application of this principle, the true wealth of the asanas will present itself to the adept.

4. *Continence* (**brahmacharya**) and 'the will to direct all bodily and mental energies towards reality' (*Hatha prdipika*) implies that degree of physical and mental concentration necessary for the proper holding of a pose. All energies should be channelled towards serving the inner spirit as opposed to the ego; likewise to imparting knowledge for the service of others and not for self-glorification.

5. *Non-greed* (**agarigraha**) - the urge to develop within oneself the patience to master one's practice with pure dedication and a rejection of all personal rewards. Non-hoarding: not to take anything without working for it, be satisfied with what happens.

Niyama

Finer law: more spiritual; the ones humanity is not ready to follow. Personal ethical code, again has five principles for application to teaching and practising. These rules require more awakened and positive consciousness.

1. *Purity* (**saucha**) of the body through the studying and practice of the asanas . . . and by this stimulating the physiological functions, one purifies the body and mind so that harmony, balance and self-control can be attained as a manifestation of God within oneself. To see virtues in others and not their faults.

2. *A state of tranquillity* (**santosa**) is essential for the concentration, mental stillness and physical stability essential for successful practice.

3. **Tapas** - *the constant effort* to achieve steadiness and strength in the postures . . . to remain calm through the discomforts and the rewards, the disappointments of practice . . . to keep on practising in a humble and unselfish manner. To work without selfish motive and hope of rewards.

4. *Study* (**svadyaya**), observe and understand with an enquiring and open mind . . . to work at every move and mood oneself but under the guidance of a teacher . . . and by so doing, gradually to learn to know oneself. To read one's own book of life.

5. *Devotion to God* (**isvara pranidhana**) - the realisation of the union between the individual soul and the universal spirit, inspired by devotional practice and constant awareness that ultimately our supreme teacher is God within ourselves. In that final state of joy, the practice takes the shape of prayer where each movement, each vibration of the skin, each instance of stillness, each breath, each harmonisation - all are a manifestation of the spirit of God on the one hand and on the other an act of worship.

Pranayama

If during practice, the breath is used properly, in harmony with the physical quality of the posture, the life-force within oneself will be controlled and pranayama (breath) and asana (posture) will become an integral part of each other and not two separate entities.

Pratyahara

This is that control of the senses which brings liberation necessary for the proper understanding of the postures and the self. Taken further, pratyahara is withdrawal of the senses from the pleasure of the senses - such as not allowing the pose to become sensuous. If yoga is practised with the right spirit of devotion, the senses are automatically kept under control and a state of oneness ensues.

Dharana

Concentration during practice should be refined to the point where there is no room for the ego and where each aspect of the posture is analysed and lived in full awareness.

Dhyana

This sustained concentration, together with the strength and harmony acquired during yoga practice greatly facilitates the achieving of a state of meditation. On this respect, meditation can be seen as a transcendence from the physical and mental preparation embodied in yoga. A state of immeasurable joy may result. This is *samadhi* . . . a glimpse of divine light which can go before it is recognised . . . which defies description and which is hence best left to the deeper silence of one's heart.

*Yoga is the method by which the restless
mind is calmed and the energy directed into
constructive channels. As a mighty river, when properly
harnessed by dams and canals, creates a vast reservoir
of water, prevents famine and provides abundant power
for industry; so also the mind, when controlled,
provides a reservoir of peace and generates
abundant energy for human uplift.*

B. K. S. IYENGAR'S *LIGHT ON YOGA*

Traditional version

1. *The Lord is my shepherd; I shall not want.*
2. *He maketh me to lie down in green pastures; He leadeth me beside the still waters.*
3. *He restoreth my soul; He leadeth me in the paths of righteousness for His name's sake.*
4. *Yea, though I walk through the valley of the shadow of death, I will fear no evil; for Thou art with me; Thy rod and Thy staff they comfort me.*
5. *Thou preparedst a table before me in the presence of mine enemies; Thou annointest my head with oil, my cup runneth over;*
6. *Surely goodness and mercy shall follow me all the days of my life; and I will dwell in the house of the Lord for ever.*

APPENDIX 2

MODERN VERSION OF 23RD PSALM

The 23rd Psalm was the outpouring of a frightened and lonely shepherd several thousand years ago. It is now sung as a cosy reassurance to seductively beautiful music but bears little relation to our modern belief that we are co-creators with God of an abundant life which he promised to our society, the rest of the world and future generations through transforming love.

St Francis prayed that he might be 'a channel of your peace (love)'. Mother Theresa (quoting Theresa of Avila) pointed out that Christ has no hands on earth but our hands. Surely today we should be praying something like this:

Modern version

1. *Christ is my inspiration and strength.*
2. *He enables me to act wisely and to find an inner stillness.*
3. *He renews my energy and opens my eyes to a new awareness.*
4. *Even when I am suffering pain and sorrow I can trust in a love which flows through our community, as I hope they can find your love in me.*
5. *I have no enemies but I am prepared to cook a meal and forgo my leisure if it can heal broken relationships.*
6. *Christ promised abundant life through transforming love. May we be able to convey this immense joy to present and future generations.*

FOOTNOTES

1. I owe this information to Jeanne Achterberg in her book *Woman as Healer*. Shambhala, 1991.

2. The book of *Genesis*.

3. This is a symbol widely used by many religions signifying the union of Heaven and Earth.

4. Sarita Chawla's quotes are from an unpublished book with Linda Booth Sweeney 'The Emergence of Wise Woman: A Learning Chronicle'.

5. Susan Langer. *Philosophy in a New Key*. Harvard University Press, 1942.

6. *Raising Cain. Protecting the Emotional Life of Boys* by Dan Kindlon PhD and Michael Thompson PhD.

7. *How to Think Like Leonardo de Vinci. Seven Steps to Genius* by Michael Gelb. Ballantine, 1999.

8. Professor Greenfield, Director of the Royal Institute of Great Britain.

9. Dr Francine Benes, Director of the Harvard Brain Tissue Research Centre.

10. *Fount of Age*. Betty Frieden. Jonathan Cape, 1993.

11. *If we're so in Love, Why aren't we happy?* Susan Page. Piatkus, 2002.

12. University of the Third Age, The Third Age Trust, 26 Harrison St, London WCIH 8JG . Tel 020 7637 8838

13. Methodism had grown up in the eighteenth century under the leadership of John Wesley (1703 - 1791). At the beginning of the Industrial Revolution he wanted to bring the true meaning of Christianity into daily life. John recognised the need for a discipline of prayer and Bible study (which is why they were called 'Methodists'). He thought this could be the foundation for 'Christian perfection' which would manifest as a transforming love. His brother Charles (1707 -1788) was an accomplished musician and wrote over two thousand hymns.

14. This was primarily a logically linguistic philosophy, prevalent in Oxford at the time, which was an excellent intellectual exercise but had little direct relevance to the way we lead our lives.

15. The eucharist is a Christian rite in which bread and wine are shared according to Christ's instructions 'that we all may be one in him'.

16. The Apostles' creed is a statement of Christian belief formulated in the mindset of the fifth century.

17. The Wren cafe is part of the St James' church complex.

18. Beverley Martin is a healer who founded the Healing Ministry of St James'.

19. Ursula works in the business and professional fields as a counsellor aiming at emotional and attitudinal healing. Kate, with her husband Jack, had run a 'New Dimensions Centre' on the south coast and after his sudden death was later to run a retreat house on the Isle of Skye.

20. Frances Moore Lappe. *Diet for a Small Planet*. Ballantine Books, 1971.

21. Frederica Chapman. *A Girl's Gateway to Womanhood: Guidebook for Girls, parents and Mentors in two parts - Part 1 Girls - Part 2 Mothers and Mentors* US$18.00 Veronica Publishing, PO Box 7555, Portland, Maine (207-828-1200) (May soon be available on Amazon).

22. More can be found about this in Paul Hawken's book *Blessed Unrest* and in the trailer to a film being made called *The Shift* (www.the shift.co./trailer).

BIBLIOGRAPHY

Some of the many books which have relevance

Abbott, Edwin A. *Flatland.* One World Publications. 1994.

Achterberg, Jeanne. *Woman as Healer.* Shambhala Publications, 1991.

Albury, Nicholas/ Elliott, Gill/ Elliott, Joseph (Editors). *The Natural Death Handbook.* Virgin, 1993. 4th Edition. The Natural Death Centre, London, 2003.

Anderson, B.S. and Zinsser, J. P. *A History of their own. Women in Europe.* Harper and Rowe, 1988.

Armstrong, Karen. *The Great Transformation.* Alfred Knopf, 2006.

Armstrong, Karen. *A History of God.* Mandarin, 1993.

Armstrong, Karen. *Twelve Seps to a Compassionate Life.* Knopf, 2010.

Artresse, Lauren. *Walking a Sacred Path.* Riverhead Books, 1995.

Assagioli, Roberto. *Psychosynthesis.* Psychosynthesis Research Foundation, 1965.

Baldwin, Christina. *Calling the Circle.* Bantam, 1994.

Bancroft, Anne. *Twentieth Century Mystics and Sages.* Arkana, 1976.

Bancroft, Anne. *Weavers of Wisdom. Women Mystics of the Twentieth Century.* Arkana, 1989.

Bancroft, Anne. *The Spiritual Journey.* Element Books, 1991.

Baring, Anne and Cashford, Jules. *The Myth of the Goddess. Evolution of an Image.* Penguin Arkana, 1992.

Baring, Anne and Harvey, Andrew. *The Divine Feminine.* Godsfield Press, 1996.

Berry, T. *Dream for the Earth.* San Francisco Sierra Club, 1988.

Bolen, Jean Shinoda. *Crones Don't Whine.* Conari Press, 1997.

Bolen, Jean Shinoda. *The Millionth Circle.* Conari Press, 1999.

Brennan, Barbara Ann. *Hands of Light.* Bantam, 1987.

Brown, Gabrielle. *The New Celibacy.* McGraw Hill, 1980.

Capra, Fritjof. *The Web of Life*. Flamingo, 1996.

Chapman, Frederica. *A Girl's Gateway to Womanhood: Guidebook for Girls, parents and Mentors in two parts. Part 1 Girls. Part 2 Mothers and Mentors*. Veronica Publishing, PO Box 7555, Portland, Maine 04102-7555.

Clarke, C. J. S. *Reality through the Looking Glass*. Floris, 1996.

Chopra, Deepak. *Ageless Body. Timeless Mind*. Rider, 1993.

Dalai Lama, His Holiness the. *The Good Heart*. Rider, 1996.

Dass, Ram. *Grist for the Mill*. Unity Press, 1976.

Dawes, Dolley, Isaksen. *The Quest*. O Books, 2005.

De Beauvoir, S. *The Second Sex*. Translated by H. M. Parshley, Alfred A. Knopf, 1953.

Dowd, Michael. *Thank God for Evolution. How the Marriage of Science and Religion Will Transform your Life and our World*. Council Oak Books, 2007.

Castillejo, Irene Claremont de. *Knowing Woman*. Shambhala, 1990.

Chardin, Pierre Teilhard de. *Let me Explain*. Fontana, 1970.

Chardin, Pierre Teilhard de. *The Future of Man*. Collins, 1964.

Chardin, Pierre Teilhard de. *The Phenomenon of Man*. Harper, 1976.

Chardin, Pierre Teilhard de. *The Divine Milieu*. Harper, 2001.

Engel, Beverly. *Women Circling the Earth*. Health Communications Inc., 2000.

Ferguson, Marilyn. *The Aquarian Conspiracy*. Granada, 1981.

Ferman, Robert. *Grassroots Spirituality*. Imprint Academic, 2004.

Ferrucci, Piero. *What We May Be*. Turnstone Press, 1982.

Friedan, Betty. *The Fount of Age*. Jonathan Cape, 1993.

Fromm, Erich. *The Art of Loving*. Mandala, Unwin, 1957.

Gelb, Michael. *How to Think like Leonardo da Vinci*. Ballantine, 1999.

Goldsmith, Joel. *The Thunder of Silence*. Harper & Rowe, 1961.

Goodison, Lucy. *Moving Heaven and Earth*. Pandora, 1992.

Goleman, Daniel. *Emotional Intelligence*. Bloomsbury, 1996.

Griffiths, Bede. *A New vision of Reality*. Fount, William Collins, 1989.

Griffiths, Bede. *The Marriage of East and West*. William Collins, 1982.

Griscom, Chris. *Feminine Fusion*. A Fireside Book, Shambhala, 1991.

Harvey, Andrew. *Hidden Journey*. Rider, 1991.

Hawken, Paul. *Blessed Unrest*. Penguin Books, 2007.

Heelas, Paul and Woodhead, Linda. *The Spiritual Revolution*. Blackwell Publishing, 2005.

Hildegard of Bingen. *The Illuminations of Hildegard of Bingen*. Introduction by Matthew Fox, Santa Fe Bear and Co., 1985.

Jampolsky, Gerald. *Love is Letting Go of Fear*. Celestial Arts, 1979.

Jenkins, Elizabeth. *Initiation*. Putnam, 1997.

Johnston, William. *Silent Music*. Collins, 1974.

Johnston, William. *The Inner Eye of Love*. Collins, 1978.

Lipton, Bruce and Baerman, Steve. *Spontaneous Evolution. Our Positive Future*. Hay House, 2011

Kindlon, Dan and Thompson, Michael. *Raising Cain. Protecting the Emotional Life of Boys*. Michael Joseph, 1999.

King, Ursula. *The Spirit of One Earth*. Paragon House, 1989. Rider, 1993.

King, Ursula. *Towards a New Mysticism*. Collins,1980.

King, Ursula. *The Search for Spirituality*. Bluebridge, 2008.

Langer, Susan. *Philosophy in a New Key*. Harvard University Press, 1942.

Laszlo, Ervin. *You can Change the World*. Positive News Publishing Ltd, 2002.

LeShan, Lawrence. *Cancer as a Turning Point*. Gateway Books, 1990.

Leonard, Alison. *Telling our Stories*. Darton Longman and Todd, 1995.

Macey, Joanna. *Widening Circles*. New Society Publishers, 2000.

Matthews, Caitlin. *Sophia*. The Aquarian Press, 1992.

Maslow, Abraham. *Towards a New Psychology of Being*. Insight, 1962.

Maslow, Abraham. *The Farther Reaches of Human Nature.* Penguin, an Esalen Book, 1972.

McCain, Marian. *Elderwoman.* Findhorn, 2002.

McCain, Marian. *Transformation Through the Menopause.* Bergin and Garvey, 1991.

McCain, Marian. *Green Spirit: Path to a New Consciousness.* O Books 2010.

McTaggart, Lynne. *The Field.* Element, 2003.

Miller, Jean Baker. *Towards a New Psychology of Women.* Penguin, 1976.

Milner, Marion. *Eternity's Sunrise. A Way of Keeping a Diary.* Virago, 1987.

Moore Lappe, Frances. *Diet for a Small Planet.* Ballantine Books, 1971.

O'Donohue, John. *Anam Cara.* Bantam, 1997.

O'Murchu, Diarmuid. *Adult Faith. Growing in Wisdom and Understanding.* Orbis Books USA, 2010.

Page, Susan. *If we're so in Love Why aren't we Happy?* Piatkus, 2002.

Perkins, Elizabeth. *Exploring New Paths.* Midlife and Menopause Project, 11 Exton Road, Sherwood, Nottingham NG5 IHA, 2004

Perkins, Elizabeth. *JourneysThrough Menopause.* Midlife and Menopause Project (as above), 2004.

Quillian, Susan. *The Relate Guide to Staying Together.* Vermilion, 1996.

Rowe, Dorothy. *Time on Our Side.* Harper Collins, 1994.

Roszak, Theodore. *Person/Planet.* Granada, 1975.

Russell, Peter. *The Awakening Earth.* Ark Paperbacks, 1985.

Russell, Peter. *The White Hole in Time.* Harper Collins, 1993.

Smith, Adrian. *The God Shift.* New Millennium, 1994.

Smith, Adrian. *A Reason for Living and Hoping.* St Paul's Press, 2002.

Somers, Barbara and Brown, Ian Gordon (Ed. Marshall, Hazel). *Journey in Depth.* Archive Publishing, 2002.

Shuttle, Penelope and Redgrove, Peter. *The Wise Wound.* Paladin, 1978.

Snow, Kimberley. *Keys to the Open Gate.* Conari Press, 1994.

Tacey, David. *The Spirituality Revolution.* Brunner-Routledge, 2004.

Taylor, Allegra. *I Fly Out with Bright Feathers.* Fontana, 1987.

Tolle, Eckhart. *The Power of Now.* Hodder and Stoughton, 2001.

Watts, June. *Circle Dancing.* Green Magic, 2006.

Wilbur, Ken. *A Brief History of Everything.* Shambala, 1996.

Williamson, Marianne. *A Return to Love - Reflections on the Principles of a Course in Miracles.* Thorsons, London, 1992.

Yardley, Lucinda (Editor). *God in All Worlds.* An anthology of contemporary spiritual writing. Vintage, 1996.

Useful Websites

www.sophiatree.co.uk

www.thegrange.uk.com

www.elderwoman.org

www.gatherthewomen.org

www.midlifeandmenopause.co.uk

www.storycatcher.net

www.theshiftmovie.com